A Scriptural Guide to A Fulfilling Marriage: Two Shall Become One

By
Gary Kaye Hardley, Ed.D.

IDEALS

Copyright © 1987 by The Institute for the Development of Emotional and Life Skills (IDEALS), Inc.

All rights reserved. Except as permitted by the Copyright Act of 1976, no part of this publication may be reproduced or distributed in any form or by any means or stored in a data base or retrieval system, without the prior written permission of the publisher. *For information address: IDEALS (The Institute for the Development of Emotional and Life Skills, Inc.)* at PO Box 391, State College, PA 16804-0391.

Printed in the United States of America

Library of Congress Cataloging in Publication Data:

Hardley, Gary Kaye, 1931

    A Scriptural Guide to a Fulfilling Marriage:
        Bibliography: p.
        Includes Index
1. Marriage—Biblical   Teaching. 2. Marriage—Religious Aspects
        Christianity I. Title
BS680.M35H295   1987   248.8'4   86-7175

ISBN 0-932990-01-0

Dedication

To my wife, Wilma, on our twenty-fifth anniversary,
who has grown with me through the years by
the Grace of God
and who along with me is in the process of becoming one
in Jesus Christ
through the continuing work of the
Holy Spirit
in our lives and the lives of those we love

About the Author

Gary Kaye Hardley was born in Pontiac, Michigan on December 30, 1931. He was educated at Prairie Bible Institute Academy, Three Hills, Alberta, Canada; Grand Rapids School of the Bible and Music, Grand Rapids, Michigan; Wheaton College, Wheaton, Illinois; Florida State University, Tallahassee, Florida (MSW) and the University of Virginia, Charlottesville, Virginia (Ed.D.).

He is married to the former Wilma Culpepper and they have five children and two grandchildren. Dr. Hardley is a Clinical Member, Fellow and Approved Supervisor of the American Association for Marriage and Family Therapy. He is listed in the Register of Clinical Social Workers, a member of the Academy of Certified Social Workers and is a Licensed Clinical Social Worker in private practice in Charlottesville, Virginia.

Dr. Hardley has conducted seminars in marriage and family relationships for the past eighteen years. Dr. Hardley is trained in Couples Communication Programs and Working Together (Interpersonal Communication Programs, Inc). He and his wife, Wilma, are trained leaders in Relationship Enhancement (RE) Therapy and Enrichment. Gary and Wilma conduct weekend enrichment seminars in their lovely facility in Charlottesville, Virginia. These skills training programs also focus upon using the skills in Spiritual Enrichment so the couples and families can grow both emotionally, interpersonally and spiritually.

Acknowledgements

Many people have contributed to the publication of this book. I want to especially thank the people mentioned below.

During the beginnings my wife, Wilma, and my daughter, Brenda, listened most patiently to the many versions. My mother, Virginia Hardley; my sister in-law, Dory Hardley; and my friends, Norma Hodson, Marla Cline Chambers and Betty Pittman gave me valuable feedback and encouragement.

Finding a publisher was a monumental task and three people were most helpful in that process. Nancy White provided early assistance and encouragement. Colleen Townsend Evans and Laura Hobe were helpful over and over again.

Dr. Bernard Guerney, President and Founder of IDEALS, has provided constant encouragement and advice. His friendship and sensitivity to me as an author has been one of the most rewarding experiences of my life.

To my parents and my wife I owe the greatest debt. They have allowed me to share intimate information about our family. There is always pain in that process but they have been supportive and willing to share with others. While they may well remember incidents and feelings differently than I do, they have encouraged me to share of myself which has of necessity involved them.

Contents

Preface		xi
Chapter 1	Trusting in God	1
Chapter 2	The Mystery of Marriage	11
Chapter 3	Becoming One	27
Chapter 4	Becoming One in Marriage	47
Chapter 5	Husbands Wives, What of Them?	71
Chapter 6	Sources of Help	119
Chapter 7	One in Unity	163

Preface

This book is written to persons; husbands, wives, engaged couples and others; who are struggling to understand God's instructions to married believers. You will find this book more useful if you read the entire passage of Scripture referred to in the text of the book. I have tried to use the particular translation which I believe best captures the meaning of the text. For the most part I have chosen the *New International Version*. I encourage you to use your favorite translation if you find that more helpful.

I request that you read this book prayerfully by yourself first before reading it and discussing it with your mate or prospective mate. It is my earnest prayer that the Holy Spirit will guide you in your study of this vital Christian relationship.

I believe that many of the modern day reactions to the Christian faith, believers and unbelievers alike, are the direct result of some of the popular misconceptions about what the Scriptures teach. I have observed that many marriage counselors, who are well-intentioned professionals (many of whom are, themselves, believers) dismiss serious consideration of the Biblical instructions on the marital relationship. They often observe that their clients are attempting to build unhealthy relationships which those clients believe

A SCRIPTURAL GUIDE TO A FULFILLING MARRIAGE

are based upon what the Scriptures teach. While the Bible could greatly assist couples to find healing in their relationship, this source of help is often overlooked and at times even ridiculed. Often this results from the misuse, misquoting and misapplication of the Scriptures by Christians.

I pray that my readers will discover the tremendous love of God, His forgiveness and His healing as they consider the suggestions offered in these pages. I hope that you will be encouraged to search the Scriptures for yourself. God promises us love, joy and peace. The Holy Spirit can and does provide healing. Jesus promised to answer our prayers:

> "So I say to you: Ask and it will be given you; seek and you will find; knock and the door will be opened to you. For everyone who asks receives; he who seeks finds; and to him who knocks, the door will be opened." (Luke 11:9-10, NIV)

and we read:

> "Therefore I tell you, whatever you ask for in prayer, believe that you have received it, and it will be yours. And when you stand praying, if you hold anything against anyone, forgive him, so that your Father in heaven may forgive you your sins." (Mark 11:24-25, NIV)

PREFACE

and in I John 5 we read:

> "I write these things to you who believe in the name of the Son of God so that you may know that you have eternal life. This is the assurance we have in approaching God: that if we ask anything ACCORDING TO HIS WILL, he hears us. And if we know that he hears us—whatever we ask—we know that we have what we asked of him." (emphasis mine, 13-15, NIV)

I believe that Jesus meant what He said and I believe that God does answer our prayers in His time and in His way. Often we do not seek His will and we do not claim His promises.

If you find yourself concentrating on another person as you read this book (that sure sounds like Mary, Joe, my wife, my husband, etc.), I encourage you to pray that the Holy Spirit will help you apply what you read to yourself and not to someone else. While you can change your own perceptions, attitudes, feelings, intentions and behaviors; you cannot really change others. I trust that you will not find any "magic pills" or simple formulas in these pages for solving your life situation because I do not believe there are any.

On the contrary this book intends to describe a process of growing through time as we learn to know God, ourselves and others better. I am also describing a process of discovering the will of God for our lives. I believe that we learn to know God's will as we walk in the truth that we have. In other words, God promises to meet us where we are and to lead us into more truth as we mature spiritually and emotionally. Learning to know God's will for you is a developmental process. As we shall see, it is the work of the Holy Spirit to teach us those lessons we need to learn and to bring about that growth. You cannot turn that process over to other people (Romans 8:26-28).

I have prayed as I wrote this book that God would protect me from any attempts to apologize, change, alter or explain away the Scriptures. Years ago I would not have had the courage to write this book. While I have always (since I was a little boy) believed that the Scriptures were inspired of God and that they were relevant to my life, I also knew that I was very troubled by how the Scriptures were used to teach concepts that I strongly disagreed with both personally and professionally. However, I seemed unable to get beyond my disagreements with others to a place of understanding for myself. I now write with boldness and pleasure.

Now I ask you to join me on a journey, a journey of growth. Commit your study of this book to God and pray that the Holy Spirit will guide you to accept those suggestions which are of Him and to reject those which are not of Him. The Scriptures are a guide to our feet and a lamp to our path. It is a record of God's revelation to man. It is not a book on marriage, but it has a great deal to say about marriage.

1
Trusting in God

These beginning paragraphs were written at a moment of decision. They were written at a moment when the outcome of a major personal, career and family decision was unknown. These paragraphs remain basically unchanged from the time they were written. It was a moment of intense anticipation, anxiety, fear and hope. It was a time of absolute disagreement between my wife and me.

My wife wanted and was praying for one outcome. I wanted and was praying for a very different one. It was a major career decision which would affect both of us and our desires in the matter could not be compromised. Our respective desires would not somehow be altered to be acceptable to both of us. The decision had to be made. The decision would have affected the lives of our children, our marriage, our careers and our commitments to what we both said we believed.

I found that the only commitment I could make at that moment of truth was to God. I could not make a commitment to my wife or family and even saying yes to God's will was extremely difficult. The commitment I finally made was very simple. I put my trust in God and told Him, "not my will but yours be done." Did I want to make that commitment? No, not really! I wanted my own way! I thought I knew what was best for me.

My wife wanted her own way too; she said she thought she know what was best for us. So what else is new? Of course, we both wanted our own way. Of course, we both wanted to do what we wanted to do.

I prayed constantly during that day the decision would be made. It was the day when I would hear whether or not I got the job I had applied for and wanted very much. I fluctuated between moments of "Okay, Lord, your will be done" to "Lord, help her accept you will", to "Lord, I know your will and I will accept it submissively." During these hours of intense struggle between God and me, I finally, at the last moment with tears streaming down my face said and meant: "God give me the strength to be victorious in your will. Father, I do not what to be a martyr or to survive; I want to learn more of your love by knowing and doing your will."

I later learned that my wife had prayed an almost identical prayer at the same time. I submitted, not to my wife or my family at that moment; I couldn't; I did not even want to! I submitted myself to God and and told Him so. My wife submitted to God and asked Him to help her work out the details and plans if we were to move.

TRUSTING IN GOD

She could ONLY submit to me as unto the Lord. She trusted Him absolutely. She loved me and trusted me to a degree but she knew how badly I wanted that job and she had seen me make bad decisions in the past.

I prayed that God would help us accept His will for us and to work out all of the details regardless of the decision. I prayed for peace and joy in His will. At the time I was reminded of Paul's statement about Jesus and realized that none of us have ever prayed until we sweated great drops of blood.

Yes, my pain was real, it seemed more than I could bear; but I knew that God loved me with a perfect love. How could I again and again doubt Him? Why was yielding to His will so difficult for me? I was reminded of the children of Israel. I had read those stories so often and wondered how they could doubt God again and again even after they had seen so many miracles. I thought they were really stupid. Yet, I have come to realize they were just like we are.

I had seen God move in my life and answer prayers and I had experienced His love in such marvelous ways and yet so often when a new trial came, I reverted back to my old doubts and fears just like they did. So did the disciples! Had they not walked with Him day and after day? They said they knew who He was and yet time and time again they failed to believe and trust Him.

I believe that this continuing struggle for me comes from an unwillingness to yield to God, to pray that His will be done and to be serious about it. I know that when I commit my life to Him in that way, He may well ask me to do something I don't want to do or to go somewhere I don't want to go. We know that we may have to give up some of the comforts and securities of our lives. We may have to take a stand which will bring others down on us.

This trial in my life, after all, was the direct result of taking an unpopular stand for what I believed was right and the consequences were very painful. Eventually that stand ended in my being fired and in a long legal battle against my former employer. Yes, sometimes when we do what we believe God is leading us to do, it can have consequences for ourselves and those we love. I knew all that because for two years I had been unable to obtain a job which used the skills for which I had been trained.

My family had literally been on the brink of financial disaster for two years. Our lights, water, sewer and telephone had been cut off more than once. While I said that I wanted God's will, I also wanted the time of trial to be over. In addition, the job for which I had applied and was waiting to hear about was exactly what I had always wanted. Frankly, I do not like this walking by faith. I find it scary. I had always forged my own way and now I could not do so.

In order to walk by faith, each of us must come to the point of saying, not my will but Yours be done, on a moment by moment, daily basis.

TRUSTING IN GOD

During our entire lives we must do this in order to be open and receptive to His will for us. It is a daily, moment by moment walk of faith. David wrote:

> "Answer me quickly, O Lord; my spirit faints with longing. Do not hide your face from me or I will be like those who do down to the pit. Let the morning bring me word of your unfailing love, for I have put my trust in you. Show me the way I should go, for to you I lift up my soul. Rescue me from my enemies, O Lord, for I hide myself in you. Teach me to do your will, for you are my God; may your good Spirit lead me on level ground." (Psalm 143: 7-10, NIV)

We often forget that our purpose in life is to bring glory to God. He created us for that purpose. It is not a matter of our willingness to do good works or to even fight for Him. It is a walk of obedience to what God has led us to do at this very moment in time.

> "If you love me, you will obey what I command. And I will ask the Father, and he will give you another Counselor to be with you forever—the Spirit of Truth. The world cannot accept him, because it neither sees him nor knows him. But you know him, for he lives with you and will

be in you. I will not leave you as orphans; I will come to you. ... Jesus replied, 'If anyone loves me, he will obey my teaching. My Father will love him, and we will come to him and make our home with him. He who does not love me will not obey my teachings." (John 14:15-17 and 23-24, NIV)

In Matthew 6:9-10, we read:

"Let it come the kingdom of thee; let it come about the will of thee, as in heaven also on earth." (Marshall)

Thus, the prelude to all of our prayers must be to seek the Father's will. In many passages in the Scriptures we are told to seek first the kingdom of God and then the other things will be added to us. Until we begin our prayers correctly, that is, putting God's will for us first, we cannot pray as we ought nor in faith believing. I believe that much of the time we actually mean, "Lord, please give me my own way!" when we pray and say other words.

The actual outcome of the situation of which I just wrote is almost incidental to the story. The real story was the struggle between God, my wife and me. It is a struggle that plays out in every moment of all of our lives. When we truly ask God to guide us, we must be serious and honest. Otherwise, we negate our own prayers because they

TRUSTING IN GOD

are a lie (we want our own way and not His way). God is holy and He will not, He cannot, grant us something which is not for our own good and is not in His will for us. He does not promise to do that.

The outcome of this particular episode in our lives was one in which we both came to know God better, came to know ourselves better and came to appreciate each other more. God's will became very clear and while we both knew that God's will had been carried out, it was not the decision which I wanted at the time.

The pain was very intense for me. My wife's comforting and my own faith in God's faithfulness created a new opportunity to grow spiritually. Both my wife and I learned once again that we become one in our individual and collective obedience to God. It is not an abstract idea. It is not a clever manipulation to obtain our own way. It is not based upon a chain of command or on a hierarchy in which the husband directs his wife. We become one in the Holy Spirit by our individual and mutual obedience to God. God leads each of us in His very individual way which is designed with a full and complete knowledge of us and our relationship.

Does God speak to us today? Did God speak to us in this experience? Yes, He certainly did. The decision was clear to both of us without any doubt. It was based upon the prayers of both of us (even though they were very different and actually in conflict) because we yielded our wills to

A SCRIPTURAL GUIDE TO A FULFILLING MARRIAGE

God's plan for us at that time, in that place and in that way. We both knew and we were both able to thank God for His clear leading even though it was not the outcome I wanted at that time.

As I contemplate the relevance of this whole experience, I am reminded on a very personal basis that this incident in our lives clearly demonstrates the message of this book. As believers, we submit to each other (that is, we seek for peace and harmony). As my wife submits to me (seeks peace and harmony and shows respect for me) as unto the Lord; I love her as myself and we together seek to live in peace, harmony and love. She shows respect and reverence for me. I seek to be gentle, kind, considerate and loving to her. We individually and jointly seek to yield our lives to God and to serve Him and bring honor to Him. There is an interactional pattern in which both husband and wife seek to know and to do God's will individually and as a couple.

Faith tells us that God does know best and that He cares for us. During this time of decision with all of its implications, the experience of Peter walking to Jesus on the water came to my mind many times. Did I have my eyes on Jesus or on the waves around me? I must admit that I would have sunk just like Peter because I kept looking away at the waves in my life.

At times the thoughts of blaming my wife for the outcome in the decision came to me, after all, had she not been praying against me and had she not failed to "submit to me". At times I thought

TRUSTING IN GOD

about how I might be able to manipulate the outcome so that I could have my own way. At times I thought about my personal needs and became anxious and fretful.

Praise God, however, He was with me and with us and He understood the struggle and His love is so much greater than my sin. He gave me the power to overcome! And in His time He provided an opportunity for me which was so wonderful that I would not have even dreamed of it.

2
The Mystery of Marriage

What imagery comes to mind when you anticipate a good mystery story? Perhaps you anticipate a time of suspense, a time of intrigue, a time of heroes and villains, hidden clues and suspects. For sure you do not expect an easy, transparent, give away plot. You expect that it will take time, effort and thought to uncover the story and to understand the meaning of the adventure. You probably discovered that you ruin the enjoyment of the adventure if you begin by reading the end of the story or if you skip around missing the clues, the suspense and the descriptions of the various characters, places and events. Mysteries are most enjoyable when they keep you searching, wondering and even going off on tangents only to discover they are dead ends.

A mystery is perplexing. It is obscure. It is profound. It is often inexplicable and it has a secretive quality. It is something which is not fully understood. At times it appears to be beyond understanding.

The Bible describes the marriage relationship as a mystery. In particular, the Bible describes the relationship of the "two becoming one" in marriage and one with God as a mystery. It is described as hard to understand. It is described as a deep hidden truth.

The meaning of "two becoming one" which we choose to accept in relation to the marital relationship must be congruent with the other uses of that expression in the Scriptures and it must be consistent with the other teachings of the Scriptures.

The Biblical phrase, two shall be one is used to describe many relationships. It is used to describe the relationship between Christ and His Church (referring to the body of believers), the relationship between the human body and Christ, a man with a prostitute, the relationship between Jews and Gentiles, and members of the body of Christ.

Similar metaphors are used to describe that Jesus and His Father are one. The Father, Son and Holy Spirit are described as one. Many become one when the Scriptures refer to the body of believers.

These varied uses of the phrase, becoming one or being one, shed light on the meaning of the process. It also gives us insight into what is not meant by the process described. It is obvious that if the process of becoming one is used to describe other relationships (other than just the marriage relationship), then all of the uses must equally apply to each of the described relationships (Eight Rules of Interpretation, *Divorce & Remarriage*, pages 145-153).

THE MYSTERY OF MARRIAGE

I believe that the deepest and truest meaning of this phrase, two shall become one, will remain to some degree a mystery even after our study because that is how the Scriptures leave it. However, we may be able to understand the process better and we can certainly dismiss those interpretations which do not fit all of the uses described in the Scriptures.

I believe that the Scriptures clearly teach that we, as human beings, only begin to understand God and the meaning of the deeper things of God:

> "In the same way, we can see and understand only a little about God now, as if we were peering at His reflection in a poor mirror; but someday we are going to see Him in His completeness, face to face. Now all that I know is hazy and blurred, but then I will see everything, just as clearly as God sees into my heart right now." (I Corinthians 12:12, *Letters to Young Churches*, henceforth referred to as Letters)

Furthermore, we cannot forget that it is the work of the Holy Spirit to give us discernment and understanding.

> "However, as it is written: 'No eye has seen, no ear has heard, no mind has conceived what God has prepared for those who love Him'—but God has revealed it

to us by his Spirit. The Spirit searches all things, even the deep things of God. For who among men knows the thoughts of a man except the man's spirit within him? In the same way no one knows the thoughts of God except the Spirit of God. We have not received the spirit of the world but the Spirit who is from God, that we may understand what God has freely given us. This is what we speak, not in words taught us by human wisdom but in words taught us by the Spirit, expressing spiritual truths in spiritual words. The man without the Spirit does not accept the things that come from the Spirit of God, for they are foolishness to him, and he cannot understand them, because they are spiritually discerned. The spiritual man makes judgments about all things, but he himself is not subject to any man's judgment: 'For we have the mind of Christ.' " (I Corinthians 2: 9-16, NIV)

Both of the above truths (we have the mind of Christ and our knowledge is limited) are taught in the Scriptures. They are not contradictory. They both clearly point us to our absolute dependency upon God. I encourage my readers to search the Scriptures with an open mind and pray that the Holy Spirit will give them spiritual discernment.

THE MYSTERY OF MARRIAGE

It is not my intention in this book to offer final answers or formulas for what you should do. I am describing the process of coming to know God more fully and learning how to walk in obedience to Him, step by step and day by day. God meets us WHERE WE ARE and leads us step by step to deeper truth and fellowship as we walk in the light we have.

Personal Accountability

Romans fourteen provides a clear warning to believers. This warning is critically important because it is repeatedly given throughout the Scriptures. Verses eleven and twelve clearly state that each individual is accountable to God for his own behavior. Paul is writing to believers when he writes:

> "All of us will have to stand before the tribunal of God—for it is written, As I live, saith the Lord, every knee shall bend before me, every tongue shall offer praise to God. Each of us then will have to answer for himself to God. (I Corinthians 2:15, *The Bible, The James Moffat Translation*, henceforth referred to as Moffatt)

When Paul was being criticized by others, he made the following statement:

A SCRIPTURAL GUIDE TO A FULFILLING MARRIAGE

> "I care very little if I am judged by you or by any human court; indeed; I do not even judge myself. My conscience is clear, but that does not make me innocent. It is the Lord who judges me. Therefore JUDGE NOTHING BEFORE THE APPOINTED TIME; wait till the Lord comes. He will bring to light what is hidden in darkness and will expose the motives of men's hearts. At that time each will receive his praise from God." (emphasis mine, I Corinthians 4: 3-5, NIV)

Each person, husband and wife, will give a personal account of his (her) own behavior. Before God, a husband will not be able to blame his behavior on his wife. Neither will a wife be able to say, "You, God, told me to obey my husband and I was obeying him when I disobeyed you". While it is also true that we will be held accountable if we cause our brother to sin, we will not be held accountable for anyone's actions other than our own. God holds us responsible for our own behavior and before Him we cannot project responsibility unto others. Each of us always has a choice about how we respond to the other person regardless of how provocative that person may be. One of those choices is to withdraw from interacting with persons who are abusive.

I do not believe that two becoming one means that individual responsibility is excused. Each of us is and remains accountable for our own behavior.

THE MYSTERY OF MARRIAGE

In order to grow as a couple, each person must stop working on his mate and he must work to change his own unproductive and hurtful behaviors. Each of us must learn to recognize that the only person's behavior we can really change is our own. However, when we do change our own behavior, the old pattern is broken (as long as we do not slip back into that old behavior) and the other person must adapt in some way to our changed behavior. As a counselor and as a husband and father, I have observed that the more hopeless we feel in changing our own behavior, the more we seem to work to force change in others.

Another word of caution seems essential in this regard. In my counseling with couples and families, I often discover that while one or both individuals deny that they are trying to change the other person, there are subtle, underhanded attempts to force change. Because of the denial involved, these subtle, indirect attempts to force change are even more damaging to the relationship. Open, direct, above board requests for change are both more honest and more productive.

Merging into One Personality

Another misconception of how two become one is that the two become one personality (that is, one or both lose their identity as unique individuals). If this meaning were true, then the phrase would also mean that all believers become one personality. That is obviously not true. If this meaning were true, the example (members of the human body, meaning organs, working together in perfect harmony) would be a very poor illustration of the process. I do not believe that a poor illustration was chosen. The expressions that the Trinity is One and that Jesus and His Father are One would mean that they are one personality. I do not believe that the Scriptures teach that to be true. I, therefore, conclude that the idea that two become one in the sense of one personality (one identity) is erroneous and must be rejected. I actually heard a minister say to his wife "since we are one, God expects you to do what I want you to do." Isn't that an absurd assertion? However, I have heard far more sophisticated arguments which, in effect, mean the same thing.

Enmeshment

Neither does the expression, two shall become one, mean that the two people become enmeshed into each other. Enmeshed means to catch or entangle. If we expect another person to complete us or to make us whole, we will remain hopelessly frustrated. Our personal and interpersonal growth will be stunted. Our relationship will become a battle ground! You do not become one by becoming two halves.

Expecting the other person to make you happy, to take away your loneliness, read your

THE MYSTERY OF MARRIAGE

mind, meet all of your needs, be responsible for you, help you make friends or to become an extension of you are all examples of unrealistic expectations and are examples of enmeshment.

Another way people become enmeshed is by losing their own identity. Jesus said that we were to love our neighbor as ourselves. Bruce Narramore in his book, *You're Someone Special*, discusses self love. He states: "... agape love is a deep attitude of esteem and respect" (page 38). He is referring to self love rather than selfishness or narcissism. I highly recommend this book to my readers. It is thoughtful, Scriptural and very helpful. You cannot try to please others by trying to be what they want you to be. YOU MUST BE YOURSELF! You were created in the image of God and you were so valuable that Jesus gave His life to redeem you for Himself.

If you love yourself, then you can freely give of yourself. You do not give up! "Dying to self", as described in the Scriptures, refers to "seeking first the kingdom of God" or "not my will but thine be done". It does not mean to become a nonperson.

The Bible is full of examples of how God used specific people with distinct personalities to carry out his plans. He chose a Moses, a David, a Daniel, a Ruth, an Esther, a Peter, a Mary, a Sarah, a Rahab and a Paul to carry out His plans and to make Himself known in the world. Each of these people, as we know, was a very distinct person who yielded his or her life to God. Dying to self does not mean that we lose our identity. It means that we yield our wills to His and that He becomes our Lord and our Savior. Jesus said:

> "I am the vine; you are the branches. If a man remains in me and I in him, he will bear much fruit; apart from me you can do nothing." (John 15: 5, NIV)

Does that mean that we are unimportant? Does that mean we are of no value? Does it mean we become nonentities? Absolutely not! It means that all of our efforts even to please Him are futile and unsuccessful unless we, moment by moment, say yes to His will and ask Him to give us His love and His strength. Otherwise, our motives are selfish.

Hence, we can reject the meaning of the two becoming one by becoming two halves. God lifts each of us to wholeness in Himself. We were created to be one with Him in Spirit and we become one with each other in the bond of love.

Learning as We Grow

When we see other couples or families who seem to have it "all together", or who seem to have that ideal relationship which we would like to have, or who seem to be blessed far beyond what we think they deserve; the temptation is to become angry, resentful or envious. I believe that Satan wants to discourage us by creating doubt, anger and resentment. He also wants us to become legalistic, copy cats. He wants us to become accusatory and envious. He wants to switch our concern from our own sins and failures to those of others.

> "It is to his own master that he gives or fails to give satisfactory service. And don't doubt that satisfaction, for God is well able to transform men into servants who are satisfactory." (Romans 14: 4, Letters)

James Moffatt translates this text as follows:

> "Who are you to criticize the servant of another? It is to his Master to say whether he stands or falls; and stand he will, for the Master has power to make him stand." (Romans 4: 14, Moffatt)

Discouragement is the result of our lack of appreciation for God's love for us and our lack of confidence in Him. Since nothing is hidden from God, He knows how and when to teach us those lessons we need. He also knows which learning process will bring the most glory to Himself and produce the sweetest result in us.

I have seen this so often in my own life. I would not have chosen His way. I wanted the easiest and least painful way. The only problem with my way is that the result would have been the same as the cost. I would not have grown much the easy way.

Those persons who are achieving a relationship which is growth producing and an honor to God have almost without exception been through very deep waters and have learned through pain. God disciplines us out of love (not vengeance) and He forgives us for all of our mistakes and failings, if and when, we repent and ask for His forgiveness. Bruce Narramore, in his book *No Condemnation, Rethinking Guilt Motivation in Counseling, Preaching, and Parenting,* which I highly recommend, talks about a love-motivated remorse, contrition, or godly sorrow that result from divine conviction. He is not referring to guilt feelings which he sees as a self-inflicted punishment, rejection or disesteem.

Remember Job's friends who came to comfort him and ended up telling him that he must have committed some secret sin and that God was punishing him. When God spoke to these friends, He said:

> "I am very angry with you and with your friends for you have not been right in what you have said about me, as my servant Job was." (Job 42: 7, *The Living Bible, Paraphrased*, henceforth referred to as Living)

Recall that the problem for Job was that God had pointed him out to satan as a righteous man. Sa-

THE MYSTERY OF MARRIAGE

tan told God that Job was righteous only because God had blessed him so much. Satan is the accuser of the believer.

God uses our life experiences to teach us of his love and grace.

> "And in the same way—by our faith—the Holy Spirit helps us with our daily problems and in our praying. For we don't even know what we should pray for, nor how to pray as we should; but the Holy Spirit prays for us with such feeling that it cannot be expressed in words. And the Father who knows all hearts knows, of course, what the Spirit is saying as he pleads for us in harmony with God's own will. And we know that all that happens to us is working for our good if we love God and are fitting into his plans." (Romans 8: 26-28, Living)

The Scriptures continually tell us to be content with where we are and to learn what we need to learn at this very moment and to trust God to produce His outcomes for us and in us. His outcomes for us will be that we will grow to be more and more like His Son through the continuing work of the Holy Spirit in our daily experiences. God knows what growth experiences we need. He knows what circumstances will produce growth and development.

A SCRIPTURAL GUIDE TO A FULFILLING MARRIAGE

"I am not saying this because I am in need, for I have learned to be content whatever the circumstances. I know what it is to be in need, and I know what it is to have plenty. I have learned the secret of being content in any and every situation, whether well fed or hungry, whether living in plenty or in want. I can do all things through him who gives me strength." (Phillipians 4: 11-13, NIV)

"Keep your lives free from the love of money and be content with what you have, because God has said. 'Never will I leave you; never will I forsake you.' So we say with confidence, 'The Lord is my helper; I will not be afraid. What can man do to me?' " (Hebrews 13: 5-6, NIV)

Satan wants us to look at others and to either judge them or to envy them. Both of these approaches to others are doomed to failure and disappointment. If our energy is going into repression, denial or projection, we will not have the energy to grow. We must face ourselves as we really are before we are able to grow or to advance to another place. (That is what good counseling does for us, it helps us to be honest with ourselves and with others.)

"The man who patiently endures the temptations and trials that come to him is the truly happy man. For once his testing is complete he will receive the crown of life which the Lord has promised to all who love Him." (James 1: 2, Letters)

I can so vividly recall the time when I was going through a time of great trial and pain. I so often found myself thinking that if I could just make it through the day, perhaps it would be over tomorrow. I wanted the pain to stop and the time apart to be over. "Already enough!" was my constant cry. I never found victory in that place. I found only pain and more pain. I found despair. You see, on the one hand, I was praying that God would have His way and that His will would be done, but on the other hand, my secret prayers was for it to be over now! That is why I found despair. I was deceiving myself. I did not really want His will, I wanted my own way. When I came to the point of praying that God would give me victory in the circumstances and would deliver me from self-pity, I began to sense His promised peace.

God sees into our hearts and He knows all of our secret motives and intentions. Nothing is hidden from Him. While His knowledge of us may be very threatening at times, it should give us great comfort. If God knows us totally and yet He loves us, we can cut out the defensive maneuvers we often use to hide the truth from ourselves and others. In other words, we don't have to fake it or lie about it. We can admit and accept responsibility for both our strengths and our weaknesses and trust that God will complete the work He has begun in us. Our peace and rest come from our faith in His ability and love rather than in ourselves.

It is important to understand that there are two people in a marriage. Those relationships which are in the process of achieving oneness are becoming that way because both people are yielding their lives to God. They are both achieving growth, freedom and joy because they are both seeking to know and to do the will of God. When there are problems, which there are in every relationship, they can deal openly and honestly with each other and they can take their concerns to God in prayer. Instead of attacking each other, they can pray for (not at) each other and they can go on loving each other.

3
Becoming One!

What do the Scriptures mean by the expression, two become one? How does this process take place? Is this process confined to marriage, that is, to a husband and wife? Who gives up what in this process? When two persons become one, does this mean that one of them gives up his/her own rights? When does this process happen? Does this mean that the husband's wishes, desires, "calling", work or needs control or dominate those of his wife? What exactly do the Scriptures teach in this regard?

Becoming one is used in a number of ways in the Bible. It is used in relation to a number of different relationships. In some places the phrase "two shall become one in the Spirit" is either used or implied. This process of becoming one, whatever it is, occupies a central theme in the Bible. It is described as an essential process in the life of a believer. I believe that as believers we must use Spiritual discernment when we are trying to understand the meaning of this process.

> "Be completely humble and gentle; be patient, bearing with one another in

love. Make every effort to keep the UNITY OF THE SPIRIT through the BOND OF PEACE. There is one body and one Spirit—just as you were called to one hope when you were called—one Lord, one faith, one baptism; one God and Father of all, who is over all and in all." (emphasis mine, Ephesians 4: 2-6, NIV)

This Scriptural passage is representative of the many such descriptions of "Oneness" in the Spirit as used in the Scriptures. The meaning of the phrase "two become one" when it is referring to "one in the Spirit" is clearly given in this text. The meaning is that of unity in the Holy Spirit. As we shall see, this usage is the one which predominates the Biblical use of the phrase "two become one" when it refers to the marriage relationship. The other references will be discussed later in this chapter.

Becoming one in unity is a walk of faith. It is the high road! It is a walk of inner peace and joy. It is a daily walk with Jesus Christ, the author and finisher of our faith. It is the road to true freedom. It can be a personal, vital, living reality for every believer. Consider I Peter 5: 7-11 which reads as follows:

"Cast all your anxiety on him because he cares for you. Be self-controlled and alert. Your enemy the devil prowls around like a roaring lion looking for someone to devour. Resist him, standing firm in the faith, because you know that your brothers throughout the world are undergoing the same kind of sufferings. And the God of all grace, who called you to his eternal glory in Christ, after you have suffered a little while, will himself restore you and make you strong, firm and steadfast. To him be the power for ever and ever. Amen." (NIV)

In Chapter Two, I discussed what it does not mean to become one. Two people do not become one identity or personality. Two people do not become enmeshed (entangled) into each other. Two people do not become one by becoming two halves. Neither loses freedom nor individuality. In fact, I believe that the Bible teaches that both persons (husband and wife) find true freedom. The two, husband and wife, become a team walking together in obedience to God. In obedience to God, I believe that the Scriptures teach that the couple assumes certain God appointed interactional patterns so that the couple can live together in harmony with each other and can become a blessing to those around them.

Actually, I believe that one of the problems today in marriage and family life is that roles have become so confused that everyone is waiting for the other person to act. While a division of labor is often very helpful, today's expectations of

A SCRIPTURAL GUIDE TO A FULFILLING MARRIAGE

men and women have altered those roles so significantly that new ones need to be developed. More importantly, however, couples must learn a process of establishing the norms and patterns for themselves which are based upon the needs and responsibilities of everyone. They need to learn the skills to negotiate these behavioral patterns under changing circumstances.

Perhaps, in Christian relationships, there are God-established patterns. If that is true, then we need to understand those expectations and live according to God's pattern. As I have studied the Scriptures, I believe that this is so. However, I do not believe that they are necessarily the traditional roles of men and women and I hope that my readers will not hear me in that way. I believe that if we understand what God wants of us that both husband and wife will gain significantly in the process of carrying out those roles because each person will find peace, joy and love.

> "Come to me, all you who are weary and burdened, and I will give you rest. Take my yoke upon you and learn from me, for I am gentle and humble in heart, and you will find rest for your souls. For my yoke is easy and my burden is light." (Matthew 11: 28-30, NIV)

Just fanciful words, right? Good rhetoric and poetry, right? No, a thousand No's! This is the promise of Jesus Christ to His followers. Judging from

BECOMING ONE!

the burdens we, believers, carry much of the time—fretting, worrying, toiling, anxiety, etc.; we must not believe that Jesus can relieve us of these burdens. It is good to remind ourselves that most of the New Testament was written by people who were being hunted down, who were facing death constantly and who were hated by the world around them. It was not written in an ivory tower or Garden of Eden. Certainly, we do not often enough act as though His promise of rest is true for us today, especially in our marital and family relationships.

> "It is for freedom that Christ has set us free. Stand firm, then, and do not let yourselves be burdened again by a yoke of slavery. . . . The only thing that counts is faith expressing itself through love. You were running a good race. Who cut in on you and kept you from obeying the truth? . . . You, my brothers, were called to be free. But do not use your freedom to indulge the sinful nature; rather, serve one another in love. The entire law is summed up in the single command: 'Love your neighbor as yourself.' If you keep on biting and devouring each other, watch out or you will be destroyed by each other. . . . The acts of the sinful nature are obvious: sexual immorality, impurity and debauchery; idolatry and witchcraft; hatred, discord, jealousy, fits of rage, self-

ish ambition, dissensions, factions and envy; drunkenness, orgies, and the like. I warn you, as I did before, that those who live like this will not inherit the kingdom of God.

But the fruit of the Spirit is love, joy, peace, patience, kindness, goodness, faithfulness, gentleness and self-control. Against such things there is no law. Those who belong to Christ Jesus have crucified the sinful nature with its passions and desires. Since we live by the Spirit, let us keep in step with the Spirit. Let us not become conceited, provoking and envying each other. (Galatians 5: 1, 6-26, NIV)

In order to illustrate a point, I am dividing these characteristics into three lists presented in Figure 1. I am placing the characteristics of the sinful nature which are often stressed in the left hand column and the less mentioned characteristics in the middle column.

As I grew up in the church, some of my most vivid memories are of the fights, the divisions, the factions, the arguments, the dissensions and the fits of rage (of course, called righteous indignation). I was one of those kids who always listened and observed the conversations of the adults in my life. I always wanted to know why much more than I wanted to know who said so!

BECOMING ONE!

Many Christian homes and marriages are more characterized by the second column above then the third. I am convinced that it is these "acts of the sinful nature" that are the ones most responsible for blocking us from becoming one in unity of the Spirit. The Scriptures clearly teach us that these behaviors are out of place in the Christian marriage and home.

Figure 1
SINFUL AND SPIRITUAL CHARACTERISTICS

Sinful Characteristics		*Fruit of the Spirit*
sexual immorality	hatred	love
impurity	discord	peace
debauchery	jealousy	kindness
idolatry	fits of rage	self-control
witchcraft	selfish ambition	faithfulness
drunkenness	dissensions	gentleness
orgies	factions	joy
and the like	envy	goodness
		patience

Becoming One in the Spirit

How do we become one? We become one in Spirit. We become one by the work of the Holy Spirit. As we become filled by the fruit of the Spirit, we become one. I believe that this explanation fully satisfies all the ways this expression is used in the Scriptures when referring to one in Spirit. Our lives as believers and as a couple become one in unity and love.

How does this process of becoming one happen? It is accomplished through a process of growth and development which the Holy Spirit produces as we yield our lives to God. As we pray (individually and as a couple) and as He, the Holy Spirit, prays for us; our whole personalities are being made over into the very likeness of Christ (demonstrated by the fruit of the Spirit).

> Colleen Townsend Evans states:
> "When we know we can't do anything, we let Him take over; we exchange our powerless life for His infinitely powerful one. Knowing we are completely dependent on Jesus the Vine for our courage, our strength, our love, our very breath, we make ourselves available to His Holy Spirit in that utterly dependent way that lets His power flow through us just as Christ means it to flow all the time. ... How sad that we so seldom tap into this power unless we are in a crisis. ... My search has come to an unalterable conclusion that our Christian lives are to be lived in such an abiding-in-Jesus-the-vine way that the world cannot fail to see that it is Christ in us, by His life-giving sap, who is doing the living: Not I that live, but Christ who lives in me." (*The Vine Life*, page 134)

The Holy Spirit produces forgiveness and reconciliation between ourselves and God and be-

BECOMING ONE!

tween each other. It is not by our striving, fretting or good works. It is not produced by our adherence to a set of rules and regulations. It is produced not so much by what we do NOT DO but by what we DO! We walk by faith in obedience to the known will of God for each of us at this moment in time. It is through His love and grace. If our lives are full of anxiety, fear, tension, striving, performances, rules and regulations; rather than freedom and peace; it is because we are not believing and claiming the promises of God.

In order to illustrate the point which I am making, I would like to present two diagrams. Since any diagram of a complex idea simplifies its meaning, I understand that these diagrams do not adequately portray either idea presented. However, I believe that it will be useful to diagram them.

In figure two I have attempted to show that each person, husband and wife in this case, becomes one through the work of the Holy Spirit. The Holy Spirit prays to the Father for each of us constantly (Romans 8: 26-28) in the will of God (lines represent His prayers for us). Each human person approaches God, the Father, through the atoning work of Jesus Christ, and He promised us that He would pray for us to His Father and that He would present us faultless to His Father (line represents His prayers for us and His intercession for us).

> "My dear children, I write this to you so that you will not sin. But if anyone does

A SCRIPTURAL GUIDE TO A FULFILLING MARRIAGE

Figure 2
BECOMING ONE

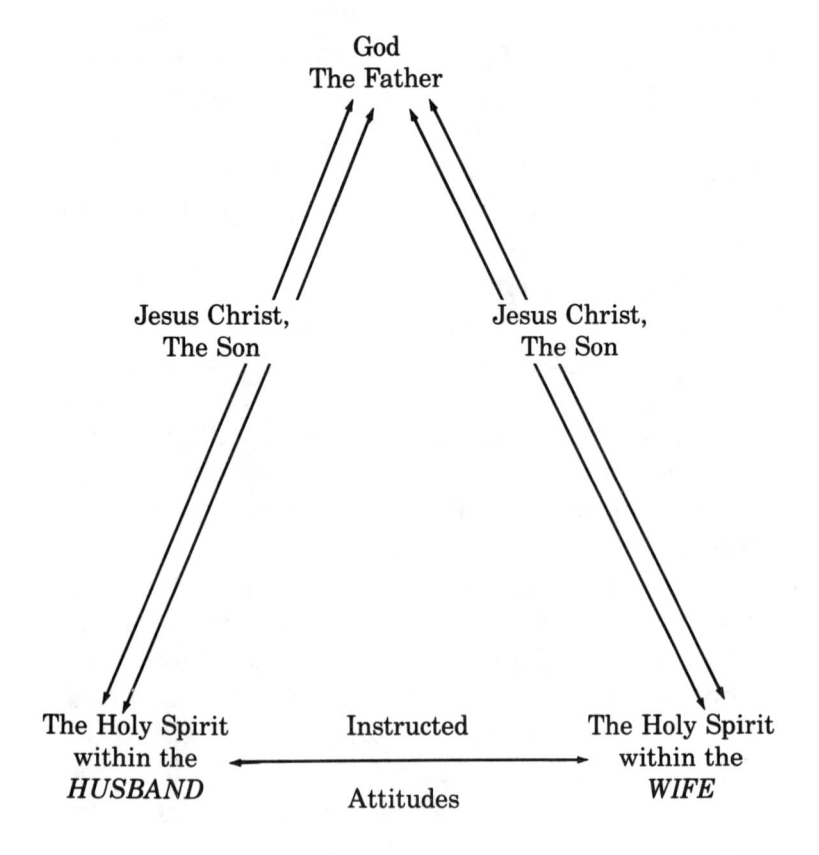

```
                God
             The Father
              ↑ ↑ ↑
             / / \
            / /   \
   Jesus Christ,   Jesus Christ,
     The Son         The Son
        / /           \ \
       / /             \ \
      ↓ ↓               ↓ ↓
 The Holy Spirit  Instructed  The Holy Spirit
   within the    ←─────────→    within the
   *HUSBAND*      Attitudes       *WIFE*
```

sin, we have one who speaks to the Father in our defense—Jesus Christ, the Righteous One. He is the atoning sacrifice for our sins, and not only for ours but

BECOMING ONE!

> also for the sins of the whole world. We know that we have come to know him if we obey his commands. The man who says, 'I know him,' but does not do what he commands is a liar, and the truth is not in him. But if anyone obeys his word, God's love is truly made complete in him. This is how we know we are in him: Whoever claims to live in him must walk as Jesus did." (I John 2: 1-6, NIV)

Since there is One Spirit, the Holy Spirit; the Holy Spirit dwells in all believers (in this instance the husband and wife). See the following Scriptures which clearly state that all true believers have God's Holy Spirit within them: Romans 8: 9-11; Romans 8: 16; I Corinthians 2: 6-16, 6: 19-20, 12: 12-13; II Corinthians 1: 21-22; Galatians 3: 1-5; Ephesians 1: 13-14, 4:30; I John 3: 21- 4:3 and 4: 11-13. The Holy Spirit within each believer, in this case the husband and wife, is in the process of making them over into the image of Christ and making them one in unity in the bond of peace. Through the work of the Holy Spirit in the lives of the husband and wife, they are becoming one.

Figure Three is from Christenson's book, *The Christian Family*. The following quote explains this model:

> "God has ordered the family according to the principle of 'headship'. Each member of the family lives under the authority of

A SCRIPTURAL GUIDE TO A FULFILLING MARRIAGE

Figure 3

GOD'S ORDER FOR THE FAMILY

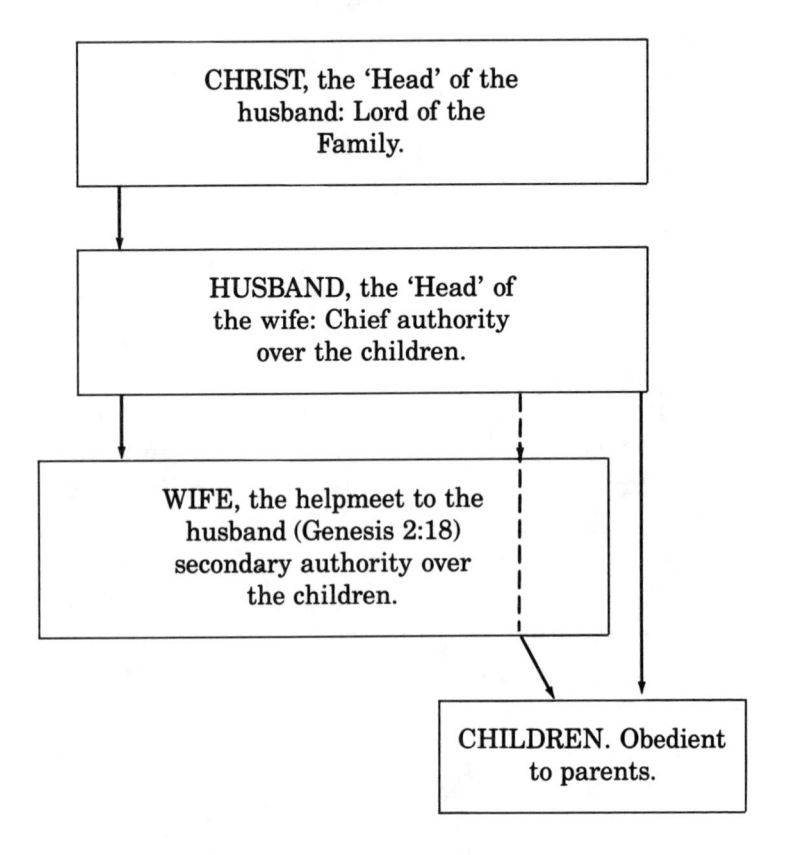

```
┌─────────────────────────────────┐
│  CHRIST, the 'Head' of the      │
│  husband: Lord of the           │
│  Family.                        │
└─────────────────────────────────┘
              │
              ▼
┌─────────────────────────────────┐
│  HUSBAND, the 'Head' of         │
│  the wife: Chief authority      │
│  over the children.             │
└─────────────────────────────────┘
              │
              ▼
┌─────────────────────────────────┐
│  WIFE, the helpmeet to the      │
│  husband (Genesis 2:18)         │
│  secondary authority over       │
│  the children.                  │
└─────────────────────────────────┘
              │
              ▼
        ┌──────────────────────┐
        │  CHILDREN. Obedient  │
        │  to parents.         │
        └──────────────────────┘
```

the 'head' whom God has appointed. The husband lives under the authority of Christ and is responsible to Christ for the leadership and care of the family. The wife lives under the authority of her husband, and is responsible to him for

BECOMING ONE!

> the way she orders the household and cares for the children. The children live under the authority of both parents. The authority over the children, however, remains essentially one. The dotted line indicates that the authority of the mother is a derived authority. She exercises authority over the children on behalf of and in place of her husband. This has great practical significance for a relationship between mother and children, which we will bring out in a following chapter."

I believe that Mr. Christenson's suggested family structure creates a hierarchy which is counterproductive to the growth and development of family members. Rather than describing this as the "Christian family", I would call it an authoritarian family. I do not believe that this structure is supported by the Scriptures and, in fact, I believe that it is contradicted by several essential Biblical doctrines.

First and foremost, I believe that it violates one of the most essential Biblical teachings about Jesus Christ. In I Timothy we read the following:

> "For there is one God and one Mediator between God and men, the man Christ Jesus, who gave himself as a ransom for all men—the testimony given in its proper time." (2: 5-6, NIV)

A SCRIPTURAL GUIDE TO A FULFILLING MARRIAGE

An even fuller statement in this regard is found in Hebrews 8: 11-13, 9: 15 and 12:24. The word men means mankind, not the male of the human race. These Scriptures clearly enunciate that each human person—man, woman, husband, wife, child—approaches God directly through Christ Jesus alone. He does not deal through mediators other than Jesus Christ.

While it is true that God uses other human being to support us, to discipline us, to encourage us, etc.; He does not approach us nor do we approach Him through third persons. Each of us—man, woman, husband, wife, child—can only approach God through the atoning work of Jesus Christ.

In fact, the more I thought about Christensen's concept the more disturbed I became both spiritually and professionally. It appears to me that Jesus, Himself, might well turn this system upside down when it comes to spiritual knowledge and faith! He says:

> "Anyone who will not receive the kingdom of God like a child will never enter it." (Mark 18: 17 and Mark 10: 14-16, NIV)

> "At that time Jesus said, 'I praise you, Father, Lord of heaven and earth, because you have hidden these things from the wise and learned, and revealed them to little children. Yes, Father, for this was

BECOMING ONE!

your good pleasure." (Matthew 11: 25-27, NIV)

Secondly, the instructions given to women and to children are given to them directly in the Scriptures and not through husbands or fathers.

"Children, obey your parents" (Ephesians 6: 1, NIV) is an example of this principle. This is also clearly the case with wives. The text in I Peter 3: 1 is the best and clearest example of this principle. Marshall interprets the Greek word used in the text to mean "submitting yourselves" (*The RSV Interlinear Greek-English New Testament*, page 915, henceforth referred to as Interlinear), and this meaning is consistent with all of the other such references to wives being in submission to their husbands.

While there are many additional Scriptures which contradict Mr. Christenson's idea, I will give only a few of them.

> "In the Lord, however, woman is not independent of man, nor man independent of woman. For as woman came from man, so also man is born of woman. But everything comes from God. (I Corinthians 11: 11-12, NIV)

> "Jesus replied, 'You are in error because you do not know the Scriptures or the power of God. At the resurrection people will neither marry nor be given in mar-

riage; they will be like angels in heaven.'" (Matthew 22: 29-30, NIV)

"There is neither Jew nor Greek, slave nor free, male nor female; for you are all one in Christ Jesus." (Galatians 3: 28, NIV)

"Husbands, in the same way be considerate as you live with your wives, and treat them with respect as the weaker partner and as heirs with you of the gracious gift of life, so that nothing will hinder your prayers." (I Peter 3: 7, NIV)

Marshall interprets this as "Husbands likewise, dwelling together according to knowledge as with a weaker vessel the female, assigning honour as indeed CO-HEIRS of the grace of life . . ." (emphasis mine, Ibid)

We are all equal before God. The Scriptures clearly teach us that there is only one mediator between God and mankind. The mediator is Jesus Christ. I do not believe that the Scriptures teach any hierarchical system for the family or for the marriage relationship. In fact, the most *dysfunctional* families I see in my marriage counseling practice are those families structured in this way. Those families are frequently filled with anger, resentment, inequality and power struggles (mostly subtle undercover ones). The children are often very discontented and rebellious. The children often assume that God agrees with their parents handling of them, even when it is abusive (For instance, God and Dad believe that I am bad). I have often seen this kind of structure result in alienation not only between parents and their children but also between the child (as soon as he or she is old enough) and the love of God. I believe that this idea of a hierarchy is not only unscriptural but that it is destructive to healthy family life and to relationships. The meaning of submission, as I believe it is taught in the Scriptures, will be discussed in the chapter four.

God does not turn the work of the Holy Spirit in our lives over to other persons, not even to fathers or husbands. He told his disciples as much when they pushed the children aside and wrongly assumed that He did not have time for them. He said that we should let the little children come to him and forbid them not, for of such were the kingdom of heaven.

Becoming One Sexually

The second use of the expression "two shall become one" is used to refer to one in the flesh. What does this mean? I believe that it is used in two ways as I will try to show by the context of the reference, itself. The first use refers to sexual intercourse. Consider these verses which are representative of the other passages in the Bible.

> "Have you realized the almost incredible fact that your bodies are integral parts of Christ Himself? Am I then to take parts

A SCRIPTURAL GUIDE TO A FULFILLING MARRIAGE

> of Christ and join them to a prostitute? Never! Don't you realize that when a man JOINS himself to a prostitute he makes with her a PHYSICAL UNITY? For, God says, 'the two shall be one flesh.' On the other hand the man who joins himself to God is one with Him in Spirit. AVOID SEXUAL LOOSENESS LIKE THE PLAGUE! Every other sin that a man commits is done outside his own body. Have you forgotten that your body is the TEMPLE OF THE HOLY SPIRIT, Who lives in you, and that you are not the owner of your own body? You have been bought, and at what a price! Therefore bring glory to God both in your body and your spirit, for they both belong to Him." (Emphasis mine, I Corinthians 6: 15-20, Letters)

Here the meaning seems very clear. In this case, you become one in the flesh by the act of sexual intercourse.

> "The Lord God said, 'It is not good for man to be alone. I will make a helper suitable for him.' ... But for Adam no suitable helper was found. So the Lord God caused the man to fall into a deep sleep; and while he was sleeping, he took one of the man's ribs and closed up the place with flesh. Then the Lord God

BECOMING ONE!

made a woman from the rib he had taken out of the man. The man said, 'This is now bone of my bone and flesh of my flesh; she shall be called 'woman,' for she was taken out of man.' For this reason a man will leave his father and mother and be UNITED to his wife, and they will become one flesh. The man and his wife were both naked, and they felt no shame." (Emphasis mine, Genesis 2: 18-25, NIV)

Becoming one through Reproduction

". . . Adam lay with his wife Eve, and she conceived and gave birth to Cain. She said, 'With the help of the Lord I have brought forth a man.' Later she gave birth to his brother Abel." (Genesis 4: 1-2, NIV)

The meaning of Cain is "I have created." This account clearly gives us another meaning of the expression, two become one flesh. Here the meaning is that in conception, a new life is formed. The sperm of the man and the ova of the woman create a new life—one flesh.

4

Becoming One in Marriage

God has given us the Scriptures so that we can understand spiritual truths. Jesus promised that He would send the Comforter to abide in us and to lead us into the truth. Jesus Christ came to reveal the Father to us and to die in our place so that we might have life. As we can see from the many denominations and different interpretations of the Scriptures, an analysis of what the Scriptures teach is an awesome responsibility. The most essential key to understanding the Scriptures is the recognition of the Holy Spirit's role in understanding the things of God. Jesus said:

> "If you love me, you will obey what I command. And I will ask the Father, and he will send you another Counselor to be with you forever—The Spirit of Truth. The world cannot accept him, because it neither sees him nor knows him. But you know him, for he lives in you. I will not leave you orphans; I will come to you. Before long, the world will not see me any-

more, but you will see me. Because I live, you also will live. On that day you will realize that I am in my Father, and you are in me, and I am in you. Whoever has my commands and obeys them, he is the one who loves me. He who loves me will be loved by my Father, and I too will love him and show myself to him." (John 14: 15-21, NIV)

"All this I have spoken while still with you. But the Counselor, the Holy Spirit, whom the Father will send in my name, will teach you all things and will remind you of everything I have said to you." (John 14: 25-26, NIV)

God is love. God and Love are the same. When we read that the husband is to be the "head" of the wife in the same way that Christ is the "head" of the church, we should immediately recognize that we are given an incredible picture of love and compassion. Jesus gave His life to demonstrate His love for us. He did not come as an authority (an earthly King), although He is, in fact, God, Himself. He came as the suffering servant. Jesus came to bring life and that life was to be abundant!

Recently as I have reread the Old Testament, I have been awestruck with God's love for His people. Within the very context of impending judgment brought on by their sin, God pleads with His

BECOMING ONE IN MARRIAGE

people to return to Him so that He can bless them instead of judging them.

> "O Israel, return to the Lord, your God, for you have been crushed by your sins. Bring your petition. Come to the Lord and say, "O Lord, take away our sins; be gracious to us and receive us, and we will offer you the sacrifice of praise. . . . Then I will cure you of idolatry and faithlessness, and my love will know no bounds, for my anger will be forever gone! I will refresh Israel like the dew from heaven; she will blossom as the lily and root deeply in the soil of Lebanon. Her branches will spread out as beautiful as olive trees, fragrant as the forests of Lebanon. . . . Whosoever is wise, let him understand these things. Whosoever is intelligent, let him listen. For the paths of the Lord are true and right, and good men walk along them. But sinners trying it will fail." (Hosea 14: 1-2, 4-6 and 9, Living)

God's instructions to us are out of love. He wants us to live in peace and joy (inner qualities). Therefore, when we read from the Scriptures that God has given certain instructions to wives and to husbands, we must understand that, whatever else is true, His love is constant. He wants us, as believers to live in peace and harmony and His

A SCRIPTURAL GUIDE TO A FULFILLING MARRIAGE

instructions to us as married believers are for that purpose. He wants our lives to be orderly and to be an example of His love in this world.

> "But everything should be done in a fitting and orderly way." (I Corinthians 14: 40, NIV)

> "For though I am absent from you in body, I am present with you in spirit and delight to see how orderly you are and how firm your faith in Christ is." Colossians 2: 5, NIV)

Since God is holy, absolutely holy, He must punish sin. Because He is love, He wants to bless us and to forgive us. God's purpose, which is so clearly shown throughout the Scriptures, is to show His love and His holiness. So when He provides a pattern for interpersonal relationships between a husband and a wife, He does so in love and in total knowledge of how He made us, male and female.

Any interpretation of the Scriptures about the marital relationship which does violence to this principle must be rejected.

I have heard the word "headship" and "submission" used in controlling and hostile ways, more times than I wish to recall. When we use these concepts to enforce our own will, to intimidate others, or in unloving ways, we have misused them and we have become destructive. God pro-

BECOMING ONE IN MARRIAGE

vides His instructions to us to bring us healing and peace.

As each of you read this and the next chapter, I especially request that you apply what you read to yourself and not to your mate. These chapters are written to aid in healing and not for angry people to use against each other.

I believe there are two ways in which an angry person can use something destructively on someone else. We can use it to judge or condemn the other person. A more subtle and even more damaging way, is to use the other person's behavior to excuse our own. We, in the final analysis, do things because we chose to do them. I hope that you will work to SET THINGS STRAIGHT rather than in attempts to prove that you ARE RIGHT.

I would like to provide another caution at this point. God's instructions are to individuals (except when they are specifically addressed to a group of persons—like the local body of believers). They are given directly to those individuals and not through other persons. In terms of service to the Lord, I have heard people saying that the husband as the "head" of his wife, determines the calling of the Lord for them as a couple. At times I have heard people claim that God expects the wife to perform those functions which her husband wants her to do for him without any regard to whether the wife believes it is appropriate spiritually or even has the talent for it. Such a serious misapplication of the Scriptures will have a very disastrous effect upon the marital relationship.

A SCRIPTURAL GUIDE TO A FULFILLING MARRIAGE

Such actions would best be classified as male chauvinism! Perhaps, the following passages will clarify this issue.

> "I am saying this to help you, not to keep you from marrying. I WANT YOU TO DO WHATEVER WILL HELP YOU SERVE THE LORD BEST , with as few other things as possible to distract your attention from Him." (emphasis mine, I Corinthians 7: 35, Living)

> "In all you do, I want you to be free from worry. An unmarried man can spend his time doing the Lord's work and thinking how to please Him. But the married man can't do that so well; HE HAS TO THINK ABOUT HIS EARTHLY RESPONSIBILITIES And HOW TO PLEASE HIS WIFE. His interests are divided. It is the same with a girl who marries. She faces the same problem. A girl who is not married is anxious to please the Lord in all she is and does. But the married woman must consider other things such as housekeeping and the likes and dislikes of her husband." (emphasis mine, I Corinthians 7: 32, Living)

In this passage Paul clearly points out that if a man or woman wants to be free to serve God fully, that person should remain single. If God is

BECOMING ONE IN MARRIAGE

truly calling your mate to a service with you, He is quite able to reach that person also. As you communicate God's calling to you and your REQUESTS of the other person, God is able, if it is His will, to lead that other person. Prayer and trust are the essential ingredients in this process. Orders, intimidations and guilting procedures are sinful and destructive.

God uses the gifts that He has given us. I am convinced after many years of pain and distress that God did not call me to do things for which I did not have the talent or the inclination. My mother wanted me to be a missionary to Africa. I never felt that God was calling me to be a missionary except when a missionary or minister would work the crowd up into an emotional experience.

I read the stories of the great missionaries and was greatly moved by their lives and dedication to God. I learned from their lives. Some of them claimed that as a result of a great spiritual experience, they were freed from sin and had a sense of peace and a sense of God's presence with them. I prayed for this kind of experience; one which immediately would transform me into a new spiritual person. It did not come! I was told that I must not be serious about it or that I had some secret hidden sin. During my religious education, a person in authority said that my will needed to be broken and seemed to believe God wanted him to break my will. He certainly tried to do so and for a long time he made my life a living hell!

A SCRIPTURAL GUIDE TO A FULFILLING MARRIAGE

God was in those experiences but not as those people thought or planned. He wanted to teach me the utter despair and pain of being abused so that I could someday minister to those who were abused. Being a counselor requires the ability to understand what people are telling you. If you have never been there, if you have not suffered as they are, no amount of book learning or training can ever substitute for "being in their head and walking around".

I just returned from vacation. I read a book which made me laugh, cry and weep. It moved me powerfully. W. Phillip Keller has written, *A Common Man's Quest for God Wonder O' the Wind*. He says:

> "And it seems that most of us are so slow of spirit, so hard of heart, so dull of discernment that we do not sense or see how wondrously the wind of God's presence has enfolded us, until we are well down the dusty road of our days. Somehow, suddenly we are startled to see that every step we took along the trail has been touched in love by our Lord." (page 13).

You see, God was quite capable of reaching me. What those people did for me was to make me angry and rebellious. I knew that God was love and I knew that He loved me. I also knew how deeply I loved Him. Yes, I was a sinner and yes, I

BECOMING ONE IN MARRIAGE

needed His grace and mercy, but I loved Him. I loved Him because I knew Him. I had met Him and He was love.

As a five year old boy, I heard the doctor tell my parents that I would not live through the night. I lived through the hell of being taken away from my parents and put into a hospital ward where I thought I was being put with dead people to die myself (they were all covered with sheets and it was dark, what else would a little boy think). But God was there. I knew Him as few do at that age. I cannot ever remember not knowing God. But then, these people were adults. They were great people of God, weren't they? They knew more about God, didn't they? Shouldn't I copy their experiences of God? Should I not have their kind of experience? No, a thousand times, No!

God healed me! I knew that He healed me. My father came to know God through that experience. God used me to bring my father to Himself and I love them both for that. I still cannot listen to my father's testimony about his conversion without tears of joy. But God had even more in mind for me! My parents used to tell me that God had spared my life for a purpose. They, I knew were right about that. Their mistake, although I am sure with good intentions, was to assume that they would know what God's will was for me. Only I could discover that perfect will. On my wedding day my father had a missionary come over and talk to me about my going against the will of God in my life (again, I believe his intentions were good). The result was that I was furious (while pretending to be appreciative) and there was further alienation rather than healing.

When I chose to become a counselor, although I did not know or sense it then, God was leading me into a vocation for which He had given me the gifts and the life training. While I found myself quickly at home and at peace in that avocation, I had to defend myself constantly. While I have had to learn a lot more about my own needs, my unresolved angers, my own need of grace and mercy; God was in that decision and He has been absolutely faithful to me.

I am sharing this experience because it is relevant to our topic. God has promised to complete the work He has begun in us. He has given us the Holy Spirit to guide and direct us. He has given us the Scriptures for teaching, rebuking, correcting, and training so that we might be fully equipped for every good work (II Timothy 3: 16, NIV). He has given us the community of believers to support, encourage and strengthen us. He bids us seek peace and harmony.

Another important observation must be made in relation to discernment and interpretation. When we study the Scriptures, we must always keep them in their context. It is always necessary to place special instructions to any subgroup of persons within the context of the whole group. This is true when there are exceptions to the general rule and when there are special instructions for certain circumstances or certain

BECOMING ONE IN MARRIAGE

groups of people. If we fail to place these special instructions within their larger context, we will often misapply them and perhaps misunderstand them because we have take them out of their context.

Husbands and wives are primarily believers. Therefore, the instructions to believers as a whole apply to them. They are accountable to God. They are led by the Spirit of God. They need the fellowship of other believers. God has promised and is well able to work in each person's life to create in each of us His image. The following verses are from Hebrews 12: 14-17 (Letters) and they apply to all believers. It includes those believers who are also husbands and wives.

> "Let it be your ambition to live at peace with all men and to achieve holiness 'without which no man shall see the Lord.' Be careful that none of you fails to respond to the grace which God gives, for if he does there can easily spring up in him a bitter spirit which is not only bad in itself but can poison the lives of many others. Be careful, too, that none of you falls into impurity or loses his reverence for the things of God and then, like Esau, is ready to sell his birthright to satisfy the momentary hunger of his body."

If we tend to blame others for our problems (not avail ourselves of the grace of God), we will be bitter and resentful.

A SCRIPTURAL GUIDE TO A FULFILLING MARRIAGE

The instructions given to husbands in relation to how they are to treat their wives are among the most demanding presented in the Word of God. God has placed an extremely high value upon the marital relationship and upon the sexual union of man and woman. He has compared it to the relationship between Christ and His church. The marriage relationship between believers is among the most beautiful, blessed relationships in the world. People around believers should marvel at the beauty of the believer's marriage. The early church was known by its love. Love should permeate our relationships.

The specialty of the marital relationship, compared to other relationships between believers, is at least threefold: the sexual intimacy experienced, the bearing of children (if that is the chosen course) and the special kind of commitment to each other and to their children. With these special blessings and responsibilities, I believe that the relationship between a husband and wife is like the other relationships between believers. Scriptural instructions to believers apply to husbands and wives unless they are specified for another sub-group of believers, such as the leaders in the local church.

God has blessed the sexual union of husband and wife and it provides a very special unity. The Scriptures describe the sexual relationship as holy and for the mutual pleasure of the couple. God clearly tells us that everyone should honor it highly and that He will punish those who defile it.

BECOMING ONE IN MARRIAGE

> "Both honorable marriage and chastity should be honored by all of you. God Himself will judge those who traffic in the bodies of others or who defile the relationship of marriage." (Hebrews 13: 4, Letters)

In the book, *The Christian Family*, Larry Christenson states:

> "In plain language this means that if one partner desires the sexual relationship, the other should respond to that desire" (page 24).

This is not what the Scripture teaches at all! In fact, such a concept is unworkable and easily becomes exploitive and even abusive. It lowers man to the level of lust and creates insensitivities which cannot help but become destructive.

The following instruction that we are not to ever regard our bodies as "an instrument for self-gratification" places the sexual union in a position far above any hint of exploitation. Rather it is described as an interpersonal experience for mutual pleasure.

> "God's plan is to make you holy, and that entails first of all a clean cut with sexual immorality. Every one of you should learn to control his body, keeping it pure and treating it with respect, and never regarding it as an instrument for self-

gratification, as do pagans with no knowledge of God. You cannot break this rule without in some way cheating your fellow-men. And you must remember that God will punish all who do offend in this matter, and we have warned you how we have seen this work out in our experiences of life. The calling of God is not to impurity but to the most thorough purity, and anyone who makes light of the matter is not making light of a man's ruling but of God's command. It is not for nothing that the Spirit God gives us is called the Holy Spirit." (I Thessalonians 4: 3-8, Letters)

Believing spouses who exploit their mates for their own pleasure are as guilty of violating this instruction as the unmarried person who does it. "Uncontrolled passion" is listed among the manisfestations of our sinful nature.

Within the Scriptures there are also stated levels of priorities. For instance, notice I Corinthians 13: 13:

"In this life we have three great lasting qualities—faith, hope and love. But the greatest of them is love." (Letters)

Love is the greatest gift. As I prepared to write this book by reading all of the references to Christian relationships and the marital relation-

BECOMING ONE IN MARRIAGE

ship, I was amazed at the emphasis I found on living in peace and harmony. Over and over again there is a strong and binding instruction to live in peace and harmony. In Titus 3: 9-11, we read the following directive:

> "But avoid foolish controversies and genealogies and arguments and quarrels about the law, because these are unprofitable and useless. Warn a divisive person once, and then warn him a second time. After that, have nothing to do with him. You may be sure that such a man is warped and sinful; he is self-condemned." (NIV)

The translation of this passage by J. B. Phillips reads:

> "If a man is still argumentative after the second warning you should reject him. You can be sure that he has a moral twist, and he knows it." (Letters)

Argumentative persons are not looking for growth and reconciliation, they are trying to be right (rather than to set things right) and this passage states that they are trying to avoid their own moral responsibilities. If your husband or wife or both of you are constantly argumentative, the Scriptures state that you are trying to hide your own secret sin(s).

"Nor let any man cheat you of your joy in Christ by persuading you to make yourselves 'humble' and fall down and worship angels. Such a man inflated by unspiritual imagination, is pushing his way into matters he knows nothing about, and in his cleverness forgetting the Head. It is from the Head alone that the body, by **NATURAL CHANNELS**, is **NOURISHED** and **BUILT** up and **GROWS** according to God's **LAWS** of **GROWTH**. So if, through your faith in Christ, you are dead to the principles of this world's life, why, as if you were still part and parcel of this world-wide system, do you take the slightest notice of these purely human prohibitions—'Don't touch this', 'Don't taste that' and 'Don't handle the other'? 'This', 'That', and 'the other' will all pass away after use! I know that these regulations look wise with their self-inspired efforts at worship, their policy of self-humbling, and their studied neglect of the body. But in actual practice they do honour, not to God, but to man's own pride." (emphasis mine, Colossians 2: 16-23, Letters)

The Scriptures are clear. If anyone is argumentative consistently and if anyone teaches false humility; they are not acting out of love but out of selfish motives. These persons are not being

BECOMING ONE IN MARRIAGE

helpful to believers who are to live in peace and who are called to live in Christ's freedom. If our relationships are full of dissension and conflict, we are disobeying God's instructions to us. These Scriptures clearly state that we are blaming others because we refuse to see ourselves as others see us and because we are trying to hide our own sin.

It may be helpful to realize that there are two basic kinds of agreements or understandings between people. Quid Pro Quo agreements are those which state or imply that one person will give such and such if the other person gives such and such. Under stress or where trust is an issue between people, these kinds of agreements break down very quickly. If one person (purposefully or not) fails to carry out his agreement, the other person often considers himself freed from keeping his. Keeping score becomes the norm and good things stop happening.

The other type of agreement is called a holistic agreement. A holistic agreement is based upon each person agreeing to do certain things to show his love and concern for the other person. According to the Scriptures we are told to act in loving ways as unto Him (Jesus even told us to love our enemies), not because the other person has done or is doing something for us but simply to show love and concern. Believers are responsible to God who always acts in love toward us. When we act lovingly, rather than waiting for the other person to act that way, we create an atmosphere of love and creative problem solving.

A SCRIPTURAL GUIDE TO A FULFILLING MARRIAGE

As a marriage counselor, I often observe that each partner is waiting for the other person to change or to begin the process of change. It is more productive for each of us to begin the process of change as unto God. Holistic agreements lead to problem resolution more quickly because each person has the power to change his own behavior. And when one person changes, the old pattern is broken (unless we slip back into that old behavior). New changes begin and become reinforced by positive changes. Holistic agreements help each person assume responsibility for his own behavior. Each person is agreeing to do certain things. He carries them out because he has agreed to do so.

When my wife, Wilma, and I were having very significant and prolonged problems, she felt that God was leading her to begin loving, positive interactions toward me. She felt that I had been cruel and that I should begin the positive interactions. She recalls wrestling with God. She kept telling God, that she would respond lovingly if I treated her fairly and lovingly. She sensed strongly that God was telling her to be the one to begin. She recalls telling the Lord that if I would just say I was sorry that she would then respond in love. But she always sensed that God was telling her to be kind and loving regardless of how I was acting. She also recalls that God gave her a promise that He would deal with me. He wanted her to be loving and kind and to reach out to me. You know, the same old question. "How about

BECOMING ONE IN MARRIAGE

Gary?" In your case, of course, you can put your mate's name in there.

She remembers that as she began to obey what she believed God was telling her to so, she sensed an almost immediate change in my attitude. She sensed that I was beginning to be more loving.

At about the same time, I went to a psychodrama workshop which was led by a very skilled clinician. Somehow (I am sure that the hand of God was upon me) I agreed to be the protagonist (the person who takes the leading part in the drama). Incidently, that was very unusual for me in situations like that. The entire group was assigned to act in the roles of those people who were significant players in my life at that time, my wife, my children and a woman friend that I had at the time. As we acted out the drama of my life, I became more and more upset. I had the worst headache that I can recall. I was holding my head and saying that it was going to burst. But they kept pressing. My kids wanted me to come home! My friend wanted to know what I was going to do. My wife kept saying she loved me. I recall that in desperation it seemed as though I literally screamed: "I don't care about that, I'm just trying to get through to my wife!!!!!!!!!!"

I could not believe my own words. Had I actually said that what I really wanted was to work things out with Wilma and to build the kind of marriage we had dreamed of so many years before. Yes, that is what I had said. And it began to

A SCRIPTURAL GUIDE TO A FULFILLING MARRIAGE

dawn on me that I had discovered the truth about what my motives really were and what I really wanted. I had felt so hurt and so angry that I was out of touch with those feelings.

You see, God was dealing with me in a way I understood at the same time He was dealing with Wilma in a way she understood. My way was public. Her way was very private, very quiet and very gentle.

Within weeks, we were together in a way that had never been true before. Before that weekend I had given up and was planning to obtain a divorce. Wilma hung on in prayer and kept believing that God was a God of miracles. And that He is! When I was hurting so badly, I shut Him out too. But God is love and the Scriptures say:

> "Who shall separate us from the love of Christ? Shall trouble or hardship or persecution or famine or nakedness or danger or sword? . . . For I am convinced that neither death nor life, neither angels nor demons, neither the present nor the future, nor any powers, neither height nor depth, nor anything else in all creation, will be able to separate us from the love of God that is in Christ Jesus our Lord." (Romans 8: 31-39, NIV)

His love is unending and nothing can separate us from His love, not even our own willfulness.

BECOMING ONE IN MARRIAGE

Acted out in the real arena of life, God moves in our lives. W. Phillip Keller (*Wonder O' the Wind*) expresses this so beautifully when he says:

> "But also, in a special sense, in my solitary moments, I knew the presence of the wind of God's Spirit pressing on my person. O the wonder of His touch!" (page 37)

Those who study human relationships and research their work are finding more and more evidence that holistic agreements which help couples and families build on positives and to act in loving ways, even when they do not feel that way, produce results. The Scriptures teach us that God loved us while we were yet sinners. He loved us and He loves us when we are not even lovable.

I encourage my readers to begin to use holistic kinds of agreements. The book which best describes this process is by Richard B. Stuart, *Helping Couples Change, A Social Learning Approach To Marital Therapy*. It is important to understand that holistic agreements must be based upon the legitimate requests (not demands) of the partners. While there are certain behaviors which will help convince us that our partner cares about us, we must recognize that some of the requests we make may well be unacceptable to the other person. Yet, if many of our requests are met by our mate, those which are not met will become less and less important. Some unfulfilled requests should not present a significant problem because many of our needs are being met. The unmet requests simply remind us of the differences between people.

I believe that there is another important idea in holistic contracting which will create the space for each person to meet his agreements on his own timetable. For instance, "I will do such and such for you each day at a time convenient to me" is an example of a healthy holistic agreement. It is often critical that we have the freedom to fulfill our agreements in a manner and at a time when it can be as genuine as possible. This is especially true when it comes to sexual and affectional interactions. Otherwise they would feel and appear to be phony and might not be helpful to either party. Powerplays are either removed or significantly reduced because the grantor is freed to give in a way and at a time that is acceptable and genuine to the giver. At the same time the requesting person does get what that person requested. Both persons needs are being met in a mutually acceptable way. Obviously, as the relationship improves and goodwill prevails, it will be easier and easier to give even when you might not want to but know that it is important to the other person. In loving, healthy relationships there is real genuine pleasure in pleasing the other person. There is a sense of "we" or oneness.

BECOMING ONE IN MARRIAGE

Equality versus Equity

Social exchange theorists believe that relationships are stable when they can be characterized by reciprocity, that is, when they show distributive justice (*Helping Couples Change A Social Learning Approach to Marital Therapy*, page 37). Before looking at the actual texts in the next chapter concerning the marital relationship of believers, I would like to point out that the Scriptural instructions clearly and unmistakably provide for EQUITY. Equity is defined as dealing fairly and equally with all concerned and free from bias or favoritism. Equality, however, describes uniformity or identical measures. Stuart points out that reciprocity implies neither symmetry nor equality but rather must be based on equity (same text and page as above). I encourage my readers to see the pattern of reciprocity which is the foundation of all of these instructions to couples.

5

Husbands, Wives, What of Them?

God has given clear instructions on how husbands and wives are to be in relationship with each other. I believe that because of our many varied and complex differences (male-female, temperaments, talents and gifts, skills, family backgrounds, education, intelligence, etc.) and because of the close intimacy of the marital relationship; God has provided a pattern for our relationships.

It is important to understand that He also gave a pattern for the local church. Why? I believe that the Scriptures teach that God wants our lives to be orderly and in harmony. He understands human nature and He understands the power of our sinful natures and the nature of our enemy, the devil. He does not want couples, families or his body (all believers) to become involved in power-plays or to be in a constant state of confusion. He, alone, knows each of us completely. He created us male and female. God also knows our human frailties.

A SCRIPTURAL GUIDE TO A FULFILLING MARRIAGE

It is essential to always remember that we remain EQUALS before Him. See I Corinthians 11: 11-12, Matthew 22: 29-30, Galatians 3: 28, and I Peter 3: 7 and see my discussion of this in Chapter two. As the Scriptures clearly show, "willing subjection" is clearly predicated on this principle of remaining equal before God. The passage does not say; "husbands demand or make your wives submit to you." The wife, an equal to her husband in every way, chooses in obedience to God (not to her husband) to submit herself to her husband (we will study what submission means later in this chapter). If this principle of willing subjection is overlooked, we are back into bondage and we are leaving the freedom to which we have been called.

For the sake of clarity the Scriptural passages concerning the marital relationship are presented in their totality and in an unusual manner. Those portions which apply to the husband are in one column, the ones which apply to the wife are in another column and the ones which apply to both are presented in the middle column. This manner of presentation is chosen so that the instructions to each partner will stand out. I believe that we have become so accustomed to looking at the behaviors of others, that we often, either through habit or intent, miss the message intended for us. We grow only as we look at our own behaviors and concentrate on changing those behaviors which are counterproductive or unbecoming to a Christian.

HUSBANDS, WIVES, WHAT OF THEM?

The following passages of Scripture are from the *New International Version* unless specified otherwise. When other translations are helpful, they will be used in the text of the chapter itself.

The first passage which we will consider is found in I Corinthians 7: 1-7 and it relates to the sexual relationship in marriage:

Husband	*Both*	*Wife*
It is good for a man not to marry		
	But since there is so much immorality	
each man should have his own wife		
		and each woman should have her own husband
The husband should fulfill his marital duty to his wife		
		and likewise the wife to her husband. The wife's body does not belong to her alone but also to her husband
In the same way, the husband's body does not belong to him alone but also to his wife		

A SCRIPTURAL GUIDE TO A FULFILLING MARRIAGE

(Continued)

Husband	Both	Wife
	Do not deprive each other except by MUTUAL consent and for a time, so that you may devote yourselves to prayer. Then come together again so that Satan will not tempt you because of your lack of SELF-CONTROL. I say this as a concession, not as a command. I wish that all men were as I am. But each man has his own gift from God; one has this gift, another has that. (emphasis mine)	

The principle concerning the sexual relationship in marriage as set forth in this passage is a broad one. I believe that we are clearly told to be careful not to read into or add to the Scriptures things they do not say. If God wanted couples to have sexual intercourse everytime one of the partners wanted it, the Scriptures could have as easily have said that as what they do say. Since the Scriptures are broad in this passage, I believe we

HUSBANDS, WIVES, WHAT OF THEM?

should leave them that way. They allow for individual differences, sensitivity, and most of all for freedom in showing one's love.

Unilateral actions on the part of either partner are inappropriate and destructive. They show disrespect and selfishness. They can easily violate the other person. Such violations are sinful. Remember, they must meet the qualifications of the fruit of the Spirit. They are love, joy, peace, patience, kindness, goodness, faithfulness, gentleness and self-control. None of those qualities allow for the selfish disregard for another person nor do they sound at all like the faulty interpretation frequently made of this passage which is that either partner should respond sexually whenever the other partner wants to have a sexual interaction. Neither does that faulty interpretation sound gentle, kind, patient or loving. What a distortion of a beautiful and wholesome instruction from the Scriptures.

Paul also states that the time span for not having sexual interactions is limited. Again he does not specify that time period, allowing for individual differences and individual preferences. He also states that the purpose of not having sexual intercourse is to devote ourselves to prayer.

Paul also recognizes clearly the power of our sexual drives. It is not for punishment or revenge. It is not for other selfish purposes.

It is also important to notice the evenhandedness in this passage. "In the same way, the husbands..." clearly describes mutuality and equity. There is always a tandem instruction to each mate in all of the passages which relate to the marital relationship. There is no hint of sexual exploitation in this beautiful passage. There is no expression of hostility toward women as Paul is frequently accused of showing. Rather there is sensitivity, compassion and just good common sense. God blesses the sexual union of the man and woman and we need feel no shame when our sexual relationships are within marriage and in love.

Notice that there is no mention of conception in this text. The sexual interaction which is described here is related by Paul to our sexual drive, itself. Saying that the Scriptures teach that sex is only for procreation is simply in error. It does not say that! This passage clearly teaches us that we expose ourselves to temptation by depriving each other of this normal, healthy part of our marital relationship.

In the last two verses, Paul talks about his own wish that everyone would stay single like himself. Notice carefully that when Paul is speaking about his own (rather than God's) preference, he clearly states that he is doing so. This is important in understanding whether or not Paul's instructions to us are culture bound and/or only for a particular time in history (we will discuss this later). Paul states that he wishes that everyone could serve God in the same manner he does. He could not honestly feel any other way! God had called him to a very special ministry and he had met Jesus in a very special way (Acts 9: 1-9). We

HUSBANDS, WIVES, WHAT OF THEM?

are also told that Paul visited heaven and was not allowed to talk about what he had seen (I Corinthians 12: 1-10). God gave Paul a very unique ministry and gave him the gifts that he needed for that task. One of those gifts was to remain *happily UNmarried.*

Paul, through inspiration, fully recognized that God has called each of us to a ministry which takes into full account the gifts He has given us. This passage and many others teach that it is up to each one of us, in response to the Holy Spirit who dwells within us, to discover God's will for us. We can be sure that the Holy Spirit will fully know and use our individual gifts, our basic temperaments, our natural drives and that He will lead us to God's purpose in our lives.

If we have the gift which enables us to handle our sexual drives so that we can serve God fully without ongoing frustration and sinful interactions, God will bless us in that decision. If we attempt to violate this principle by staying single and burning with desire, we provide Satan with an avenue of constant attack and temptation which can be very powerful.

As I became a man, a number of pastors and believers misused this text to teach that "if we truly loved God, we would stay unmarried and serve God without reservation." I recall the pain, the guilt, the self-recriminations which resulted for me from such a false teaching. Staying single to serve God with singleness of purpose and without sexual frustration is a gift from God. It is not

A SCRIPTURAL GUIDE TO A FULFILLING MARRIAGE

primarily a matter of dedication. I wanted to serve God and I loved Him very much. However, I also knew myself. I knew that I did not have this ability. A meaningful, close, intimate, affectional and sexual relationship with a woman that I loved and who loved me was a driving force in my life. I would have been a fool to disregard what I knew about myself. I would have been constantly defeated and in despair.

One of the greatest joys in my life has been my wife, my children, my grandchildren and the love I give and receive from them. Paul makes this fact very clear in this passage.

This is a beautiful passage when understood for what it says and not what is sometimes read into it. The Holy Spirit had to free me from what people used this text and others to say because I kept reading these things into the text. If you, too, have been so misled, ask the Holy Spirit to lead you into the truth. Jesus promised that He would. God has made us the way we are and He knows us completely. God has made us to bring glory to Himself! When we are led back into bondage by inappropriate advice and condemnation, we forfeit the freedom to which we have been called. God expects us to be wise and honest. His calling is always based upon His complete knowledge of us. God has given us our bodies and the Scriptures describe our bodies as part of Christ. God will lead you, as He is leading me, into the ministry that He has for us and we can be sure that He has given us the gifts for that service. He

HUSBANDS, WIVES, WHAT OF THEM?

will guide us through the work of the Holy Spirit in our lives. Remember that Jesus said that His yoke is easy and His burden is light. If it is other than that, we need to find out why. Perhaps, it is because we have allowed others to take away our freedom in Christ. He has called us to live in peace, harmony and love and He is faithful to His promises. The problem is never with our loving Father. It may well be from other Christians who would take away our freedom in Christ.

The next passage is found in Ephesians 5: 21-33 and it discusses a specific relational pattern for husbands and wives:

Husband	*Both*	*Wife*
	Submit to one another out of reverence to Christ	
		Wives, submit to your husbands as to the Lord. For the husband is the head of the wife as Christ is the head of the church, his body, of which he is the Savior. Now as the church submits to Christ so also wives should submit to their husbands in everything.
Husbands, love your wives, just as		

A SCRIPTURAL GUIDE TO A FULFILLING MARRIAGE

(Continued)

Husband	Both	Wife
Christ loved the church and gave himself up for her to make her holy, cleansing her by the washing with water through the word, and present her to himself as a radiant church, without stain or wrinkle or any other blemish, but holy and blameless. In this same way, husbands ought to love their wives as their own bodies. He who loves his wife loves himself.		
	After all, no one ever hated his own body, but he feeds and cares for it, as Christ does the church—for we are members of his body. 'For this reason a man will leave his father and mother and be united to his wife, and the two will become one flesh.'	

HUSBANDS, WIVES, WHAT OF THEM?

(Continued)

Husband	Both	Wife
	This is a profound mystery—but I am talking about Christ and the church.	
However, each one of you also must love his wife as he loves himself.		
		and the wife must respect her husband.

This passage is a beautiful description of perfect love between a husband and wife. I believe that this pattern in interpersonal relationships between husband and wife is consistent throughout the Scriptures and, therefore, is not the result of the culture of Paul's day or written only for that time and that culture. While I believe that this is true, I also believe that this text and others like it must be interpreted within their context and within the larger context of all of Scripture.

What about Abusive Relationships?

I want to make an extremely important observation at this point. I am choosing to do so at this point because there is so much misunderstanding and false teaching about submission.

A SCRIPTURAL GUIDE TO A FULFILLING MARRIAGE

Wives being in submission is described as a Biblical behavior in many popular books within the Christian community.

Being in submission, whatever that means, is an instructed behavior for all believers. Notice that this passage is introduced by the words: "Submit to one another out of reverence to Christ". Paul is addressing all believers at this point and therefore the instruction to wives in the next verse must be kept in that context. Submission is different than obedience! Children are told to obey their parents. Wives are, as are all believers, told to be submissive. We must look carefully at what submission means and not confuse it with obedience. They are not the same!

When does the instruction to be submissive not apply to believers and to wives? Are there exceptions to this command of the Lord? When we place this command in its proper perspective, we will find that there are distinct Scriptual commands which override this instruction to wives and to believers. I am convinced that the Scriptures teach us to rightly divide the Scriptures so that we are not led into error.

> "But now I am writing that you MUST NOT ASSOCIATE with anyone who calls himself a brother but who is SEXUALLY IMMORAL or GREEDY, an IDOLATER or a SLANDERER, a DRUNKARD or a SWINDLER. With such a man do not even eat. . . . Expel the wicked man from

HUSBANDS, WIVES, WHAT OF THEM?

among you." (emphasis mine, I Corinthians 5: 11-13, NIV)

These kinds of instructions are found consistently throughout the Scriptures and in this particular case, Paul is writing to all believers and his instructions to expel the wicked person is given to the local body of believers. This instruction applies as equally to married couples and families as it applies to certain single individuals. The instruction is to ALL BELIEVERS and therefore to Christian husbands and wives.

I am disturbed by those ministers and counselors who tell wives that they should stay with abusing husbands (the same concern applies to abusive wives and abusive children). Such instructions are unscriptural, dangerous and bring dishonor to the Christian church. Actually, the body of believers is told to expel such people from their fellowship and to withdraw from associating with them.

What behaviors are described in this and similar texts? They are as listed in *The RSV Interlinear Greek-English New Testament*:

> fornicators
> a covetous man
> a railer
> a drunkard
> a rapacious man

The word railer is interpreted by Gingrich as revile, reproach, and verbal abuse (*Shorter Lexi-

A SCRIPTURAL GUIDE TO A FULFILLING MARRIAGE

con of The Greek New Testament). A railer is a person who subjects others to verbal abuse, to blame, to discredit, to disgrace, to censure or to scorn.

This meaning sounds very similar to Jesus's words as recorded in Matthew 5: 22-24:

> "But I tell you that anyone who is angry with his brother is subject to judgment. Again anyone who says to his brother, Raca, is answerable to the Sanhedrin. But anyone who says, 'you fool' will be in danger of the fire of hell. . . . First go and be reconciled to your brother; then come and offer your gift." (NIV)

The Greek word interpreted as "associate" actually means "to associate intimately with" (Marshall, Ibid). That meaning takes on special significance when one is referring to a couple and especially to the intimacy of the marital bed. The common excuse of "I have a temper" and "I just cannot control it at times" is a lie! It is a refusal to deal with one of the characteristics of the sinful nature: "fits of rage". The Holy Spirit of God can and will help us overcome this very bad habit which we probably first demonstrated as a little child in a temper tantrum. It is not inherited. *It is a habit.* It is a way to force others to give into us (watch a child who is throwing one) and it is a true sign of immaturity. Counseling can also help persons find better and more effective ways to express and control their emotions.

HUSBANDS, WIVES, WHAT OF THEM?

> "But if anyone causes one of these little ones who believe in me to sin, it would be better for him to have a large millstone hung around his neck and to be drowned in the depths of the sea. Woe to the world because of the things that cause people to sin! Such things must come, but woe to the man through whom they come!" (Matthew 18: 6-7, NIV)

When I read this warning, I wonder if it might not apply to those persons who tell people to stay in abusive situations. I have experienced first hand and have seen in others the results of that advice. I believe that those advice givers, themselves, often contribute to the abuse by blocking or intimidating the person to stay in that abusive environment. If the abusing person claims to be a believer, the local church is instructed to first send a spiritual person to talk with him (her)—with the hope and intent to restore him (her).

> "Brothers, if someone is caught in a sin, you who are SPIRITUAL should restore him GENTLY. But watch yourself, or you also may be tempted. Carry each other's burden, and in this way you will fulfill the law of Christ. If anyone thinks he is something when he is nothing, he deceives himself. Each one should test his own actions. Then he can take pride in himself, without comparing himself to somebody else, for each one should carry

A SCRIPTURAL GUIDE TO A FULFILLING MARRIAGE

> his own load. ... Therefore, as we have opportunity, let us do good to all people, especially to those who belong to the family of believers." (emphasis mine, Galatians 6: 1-10, NIV)

If this restorative process does not result in changed behavior (end of the abuse); the body is told to then send several spiritual persons to see that person and plead with him (her) humbly and if they fail to reach that person then they are told to take that person before the church and to expel him (her). (Galatians 6: 1-10). IF ANY OF MY READERS HAVE RECEIVED THE ADVICE THAT THEY ARE TO STAY IN ABUSIVE SITUATIONS (see definition on page 85), I URGE THEM TO SEEK OTHER COUNSEL. Find someone who understands and will help you take the necessary steps to get out of that environment. Any advice to stay in the abusive environment is not based upon the Scriptures and it is not appropriate.

When abuse is not involved and we are not instructed to separate ourselves, I believe that we must clearly recognize another important Scriptural principle. The Holy Spirit promises us that if we are son's of God that He will complete the work He has begun in us. The Holy Spirit works from within and the Scriptures clearly teach that God is well able to complete the work He has begun in His chosen ones. The most extreme example of this is found in I Corinthians 5: 1-5 and it is

HUSBANDS, WIVES, WHAT OF THEM?

in reference to sexual immorality (a man had his father's wife):

> "... The man who has done such a thing should certainly be expelled from your fellowship! ... and I assure you as though I were actually with you that I have already pronounced judgment in the name of the Lord Jesus on the man who has done this thing. As one present in spirit when you are assembled, I say by the power of the Lord Jesus that the man should be left to the mercy of Satan so that while his body will experience the destructive powers of sin his spirit may yet be saved in the day of the Lord."
> (*The New Testament*)

Husbands and wives cannot take over the Holy Spirit's responsibility in the life of their mate. They can pray for them, they can love them, they can seek peace and harmony and they can separate from them when appropriate. God can and does keep His promises and He does answer prayer. My own marriage is ample proof of his power.

Submission

I would like to return to the text that we are considering. Recall that this instruction to wives

A SCRIPTURAL GUIDE TO A FULFILLING MARRIAGE

is introduced by the identical instruction to all believers. Isn't that fascinating? I would like to refer my readers to another text to further illustrate this essential context.

> "Young men, in the same way be submissive to those who are older. Clothe yourselves with humility toward one another, because 'God opposes the proud but gives grace to the humble.' Humble yourselves, therefore, under God's mighty hand, that he may lift you up in due time. Cast all your anxiety on him because he cares for you." (I Peter 5: 5-7, NIV)

It appears that this instruction concerning submission is used in many other relationships and, that whatever it means, it would need to apply to those other circumstances as well. While younger men are given the same instruction concerning older men and the very same word is used to instruct all believers as the one to wives, why are women and wives singled out so consistently and why is this instruction distorted to mean obedience when it comes to wives?

I have become convinced from my study of these Scriptures and from the wider context of all believers, that the expression "be in submission" means in behavioral terms that wives as all believers are to SEEK PEACE and HARMONY. They are to show humility, respect and reverence for their husbands.

HUSBANDS, WIVES, WHAT OF THEM?

> "Be completely humble and gentle; be patient, bearing with one another in love. MAKE EVERY EFFORT TO KEEP THE UNITY OF THE SPIRIT THROUGH THE BOND OF PEACE. There is one body and one Spirit—just as you were called to one hope when you were called—one Lord, one faith, one baptism; one God and Father of all, who is over all and in all." (emphasis mine, Ephesians 4: 2-6, NIV)

The instructions to husbands is that they are to love their wives as Christ loved the church. Can you imagine that? In order to more fully understand this perfect love which Christ shows to His church, I encourage my readers to review the Gospels in relation to how Jesus dealt with people when He was on earth and also to review all of the promises which apply to us today. It is true that Jesus was harsh with those persons who felt that they could merit God's favor because of their own goodness. Yet, with sinners, those who recognized their need of Him; He was loving, compassionate, inviting and forgiving. Even His reprimands were direct and loving.

Remember His look at Peter when Peter had just denied Him three times (Luke 22: 60). Remember His manner when He offered Living Water to the woman at the well (John 4: 1-26). Remember how He dealt with the woman caught in adultery and those who were accusing her

A SCRIPTURAL GUIDE TO A FULFILLING MARRIAGE

(John 8: 1-11). Remember His manner with Thomas the doubter (John 20: 24-29). Remember His walk with two of His disciples on the Emmaus Road (Luke 24: 13-32). Remember His promise to us:

> "Come unto me all you who are weary and heavy burdened and I will give you rest." (Matthew 11: 28, NIV)

His love for us is an incredible standard for husbands. None of us even begin to comprehend his love for us. We can only walk in His love, agape love, because His Spirit, the Holy Spirit, dwells in us. In our own strength and wisdom we will be absolute failures by His standard.

The idea expressed in the Scriptures in relation to "head" is one of nourishment (Colossians 2: 19). The *New International Version* translates this verse as follows:

> "He has lost connection with the Head, from whom the whole body, supported and held together by its ligaments and sinews, grows as God causes it to grow."

Phillips translates this as:

> "It is from the head alone that the body, by its natural channels, is nourished and built up and grows according to God's laws of growth."

HUSBANDS, WIVES, WHAT OF THEM?

Note the reference to growing as God causes us to grow. Again the emphasis is upon a natural growing process which is produced in our lives by God. The husband is described a source of *nourishment* (as is Christ) rather than *authority*.

As with the description of the Vine which Jesus uses in John 15 to describe Himself in relationship to us, we have the picture of life-giving sustenance. Jesus describes Himself as the Living Water, the Bread of Heaven, the Vine, the Shepherd, the Resurrection and the Life, the Road, the Truth and as a Servant. All of these metaphors indicate nourishment and life. When Jesus was asked who would be the greatest in the kingdom of heaven, Jesus said:

> "The greatest among you will be your servant. For whoever exalts himself will be humbled, and whoever humbles himself will be exalted." (Matthew 23: 11, NIV)

Jesus gave the following example to His disciples concerning His love:

> "Having loved his own who were in the world, he now showed them the full extent of his love. The evening meal being served, and the devil had already prompted Judas Iscariot, son of Simon, to betray Jesus. Jesus knew that the Father had put all things under his power, and

that he had come from God and was returning to God; so he got up from the meal, took off his outer clothing, and wrapped a towel around his waist. After that, he poured water into a basin and began to wash his disciples' feet, drying them with the towel that was wrapped around him. He came to Simon Peter, who said to him, 'Lord, are you going to wash my feet? Jesus replied, 'you do not realize now what I am doing, but later you will understand.' 'No, said Peter 'you shall never wash my feet.' Jesus answered, 'Unless I wash you, you have no part with me.' 'Then, Lord,' Simon Peter replied, 'not just my feet but my head as well!' Jesus answered, 'A person who has had a bath needs only to wash his feet; his whole body is clean. And you are clean, though not everyone of you.' ... When he had finished washing their feet, he put on his clothes and returned to his place. 'Do you understand what I have done for you?' he asked them. 'You call me 'teacher' and 'Lord' and rightly so, for that is what I am. Now that I, your Lord and Teacher, have washed your feet, you also should wash one another's feet. I have set the example that you should do as I have done for you. I tell you the truth, no servant is greater than his master, nor is a messenger greater than the one who sent him. Now that you know

HUSBANDS, WIVES, WHAT OF THEM?

> these things, you will be blessed if you do them." (John 13: 1-17, NIV)

The example of Jesus is that He came as the servant. The message of Jesus is to serve one another. He came to live among us as Love and He gave Himself for us both in life and in death. He wants us to serve each other in love. The prophet Micah responds to the question of what God wants from us in a very clear and explicit way. Micah lists several things that God might want from us and rejects them with this conclusion:

> "No, He has told you what He wants, and this is all it is; to be fair and just and merciful, and to walk humbly with your God." (Micah 6: 8, Living)

Jesus gave the same message to the people of His day (Matthew 23: 23, NIV):

> "For you tithe down to the last mint leaf in your garden, but ignore the important things—justice and mercy and faithfulness. Yes, you should tithe, but you shouldn't leave the more important things undone."

It is very clear that when God places the husband in the position of "head", God expects him to show justice, mercy and faithfulness. He also without question expects the husband to show love, compassion and understanding. The position of "head" is not for self-aggrandizement or for personal gain. It is not described as a position of power over others. It is for service, nourishment, love and compassion. It is to make sure that the needs of his family are met and that they are cared for and protected.

When a husband understands the true meaning of his responsibility as the "head" of his wife, he will humbly ask God to help him live in peace, in the fear of God and in obedience to God. He will take this responsibility in fear and trembling rather than in arrogance.

Wives are told, as are all believers, to submit as unto the Lord. The Scriptures do not picture a wife as a martyr moping around and suffering silently. They picture her as an active, willing, loving person who seeks to live in harmony and peace with her husband, her family and other believers.

Since there is so much misunderstanding about what the Scriptures teach concerning submission, I would like to examine several Biblical passages which clarify this expected behavior. The following text is one of the most beautiful ones in the Scriptures:

> "A wife of noble character who can find? She is worth far more than rubies. Her husband has full confidence in her and lacks nothing of value. She brings him good, not harm, all the days of her life. She selects wool and flax and works with

HUSBANDS, WIVES, WHAT OF THEM?

eager hands. She is like the merchant ships; bringing food from afar. She gets up while it is still dark; she provides food for her family and portions for servant girls. She considers a field and buys it; out of her earnings she plants a vineyard. She sets about her work vigorously; her arms are strong for her tasks. She sees that her trading is profitable, and her lamp does not go out at night. In her hand she holds the distaff and grasps the spindle with her fingers. She opens her arms to the poor and extends her hands to the needy. When it snows, she has no fear for her household; for all of them are clothed in scarlet. She makes coverings for her bed; she is clothed in fine linen and purple. Her husband is respected in the city gate, where he takes his seat among the elders of the land. She makes linen garments and sells them, and supplies the merchants with sashes. She is clothed with strength and dignity; she can laugh at the days to come. She speaks with wisdom, and faithful instruction is on her tongue. She watches over the affairs of her household and does not eat the bread of idleness. Her children arise and call her blessed; her husband also, and he praises her, 'Many women do noble things, but you surpass them all.' Charm is deceptive, and beauty is fleeting; but a woman who fears the Lord is to be praised. Give her the reward she has earned, and let her works bring her praise at the city gate." (Proverbs 31: 10-30, NIV)

This passage describes an independent, resourceful, loving, fully functioning person. This passage does not describe a dependent, obedient, subservient person. Along with man, woman was created in the image of God. They are male and female and they are God's highest creation. They are in every sense equal before God. One of the stories in the Bible that most moves me is the account of Jesus after His resurrection. To whom did He appear? To Mary of Magdala, a woman, a former prostitute and demon possessed person. He just said to her "Mary." "She turned to him and cried in Aramaic, 'Rabboni!'" (John 20: 16-17, NIV). Jesus did not deal with her through men! He loved her and she loved Him.

With one exception, it was women who were at the cross with Him when He died; the men had fled! There are so many examples of women walking with and serving Jesus while He walked among us. There are so many examples of God's direct encounters with women throughout the Scriptures.

Another important encounter which is recorded has an interesting prelude. The Scriptures tell us that his disciples were surprised to find

HUSBANDS, WIVES, WHAT OF THEM?

him talking with a woman, the woman at the well. And the comment is added: "But no one asked, 'what do you want?' or 'Why are you talking with her?'" (John 4: 27, NIV) It seems that today some people (those who teach the false and damaging idea of God's Chain of Command) would dare ask Him and they might want Him to talk only with men.

If what I am saying is true, why are wives told to be submissive to their husbands and husbands are told to love their wives. Why are the instructions not the same? I believe that we must understand who God is in order to answer this question appropriately. God is Love. God is Holy. God is all knowing. God created us, male and female. Therefore, whatever else is true, we can be sure that He gave us these instructions in love, in sensitivity and complete knowledge of His highest creation—mankind.

I believe that God's purpose is for us to live in peace and harmony. Our ultimate purpose is to bring honor and glory to Him. God knows, as we all know, that every couple would have significant differences and that those differences would often lead to conflict. Those conflicts, especially if public, could be divisive and disruptive. Let us look at a passage which makes many people terribly uncomfortable today.

> "A woman should learn in quietness and full submission. I DO NOT PERMIT A WOMAN TO TEACH OR TO HAVE AU-

> THORITY OVER A MAN; she must be silent. For Adam was formed first, then Eve. And Adam was not the one deceived; it was the woman who was deceived and became a sinner. But a woman will be safe through childbirth, if they continue in faith, love and holiness with propriety. (emphasis mine, I Timothy 2: 11-15, NIV)

Before dealing directly with this text, I want to again put it in its context. Paul is giving instructions to young Timothy about his ministry. He states the purpose of these instructions in I Timothy 5: 7.

> "Give the people these instructions, too, so that no one may be open to blame." (NIV)

Also note what Paul says about men who are wanting to be leaders in the church:

> "Now the overseer must be above reproach, the husband of but one wife, temperate, self-controlled, respectable, hospitable, able to teach, not given to much wine, not violent but gentle, not quarrelsome, not a lover of money. He must manage his own family well and see that his children obey him with proper respect. . . . He must not be a re-

HUSBANDS, WIVES, WHAT OF THEM?

> cent convert, or he may become conceited and fall under the same judgment as the devil. He must have a good reputation with outsiders, so that he will not fall into disgrace and into the devils trap." (I Timothy 3: 2-7, NIV)

Also listen to Paul's instructions to Timothy about Deacons:

> "Deacons, likewise, are to be men worthy of respect, sincere, not indulging in much wine, and not pursuing dishonest gain. They must keep hold of the deep truth of the faith with a clear conscience. They must first be tested; and then if there is nothing against them, let them serve as deacons." (I Timothy 3: 8-10, NIV)

Paul then goes on to refer to women:

> "In the same way, their wives are to be women of respect, not malicious talkers but temperate and trustworthy in everything". (I Timothy 3: 11, NIV)

Paul then goes on in relation to Deacons:

> "A deacon must be the husband of but one wife and must manage his children and his household well. Those who have served well will gain an excellent stand-

ing and great assurance in their faith in
Christ Jesus." (I Timothy 3: 12-13, NIV)

In Chapter five of I Timothy, Paul goes on to give young Timothy many other instructions concerning the way to manage the needs of the congregation. One of those is particularly poignant:

"If anyone does not provide for his relatives, and especially for his immediate family, HE HAS DENIED THE FAITH AND IS WORSE THAN AN UNBELIEVER" (emphasis mine, I Timothy 5: 8, NIV)

Many have accused Paul of belittling women. Is this the case? Is Paul a product of his culture and; therefore, what he says in this regard no longer relevant? I do not believe this is true as we saw in the text in which Paul clearly points out that his personal preference was that everyone would stay single. In other places, he clearly says, "for the present time". Paul also clearly states: "I do not permit" and that is different from saying "Do Not PERMIT". It is also important to remember that Peter, who was married, gives us the same instructions concerning marriage as does Paul (I Peter 3: 1-7).

I believe that the context clears up the intended message and it is the same as we have been discovering over and over again. There is an underlying principle and goal. Paul and the other

HUSBANDS, WIVES, WHAT OF THEM?

writers of the Scripture see a far more essential battle going on than the battle of the sexes. (The salvation of sinners to the WAY.) They see a far higher purpose in our lives than we tend to see. They had met the Lord and they knew that their purpose was to bring honor to God by their lives. They did not want anything in the Christian home or marriage to bring dishonor to God.

I would like my readers to recall the illustration which is given many times in the Scriptures in terms of marriage:

> "The body is a unit, though it is made up of many parts; and though all its parts are many, they form one body. So it is with Christ. For we were all baptized by one Spirit into one body—whether Jews or Greeks, slave or free—and we were all given one Spirit to drink.
>
> Now the body is not made up of one part but of many. If the foot should say, 'Because I am not a hand, I do not belong to the body,' it would not for that reason cease to be part of the body. And if the ear should say, 'Because I am not an eye, I do not belong to the body,' it would not for that reason cease to be part of the body. If the whole body were an eye, where would the sense of hearing be? If the whole body were an ear, where would the sense of smell be? But in fact God has

A SCRIPTURAL GUIDE TO A FULFILLING MARRIAGE

arranged the parts in the body, everyone of them, just as he wanted them to be. If they were all one part, where would the body be? As it is, there are many parts, but one body.

"The eye cannot say to the hand, 'I don't need you!' And the head cannot say to the feet, 'I don't need you!' On the contrary, those parts of the body that seem to be weaker are indispensable, and the parts that we think are less honorable we treat with special honor. And the parts that are unpresentable are treated with special modesty, while our presentable parts need no special treatment. But God has combined the members of the body and has given greatest honor to the parts that lacked it, so that there should be NO DIVISION in the body, but that its parts should have EQUAL concern for EACH OTHER. If one part suffers, every part suffers with it; if one part is honored, every part is honored.

NOW YOU ARE THE BODY OF CHRIST, AND EACH ONE OF YOU IS A PART OF IT." (emphasis mine, I Corinthians 12: 12-27, NIV)

This metaphor is so wonderfully descriptive of God's creative love. Some men have distorted a beautiful pattern of interpersonal relationships,

HUSBANDS, WIVES, WHAT OF THEM?

herein described, to ugliness. God intended a beautiful harmonious body and we have distorted it into male chauvinism, male dominated hierarchies and ideas like Chains of Commands.

Yes, there is sin in the world. Sin mars our lives. Satan wants us to be selfish, self-centered and to assert our own wills—'You will be like God, knowing good and evil'. It is so easy for us to distort the intent and the motive of each other and of God. It is easy to believe the lies of Satan that God wants to take away the fun and enjoyments of life. Some even claim the Bible is sexist and must be rewritten. How distorted their reality has become. Some cry that God is cruel and vindictive.

Jesus came and He said that God is love. He showed us so differently that He loves us and wants us to be holy as He is holy. We were created in His image, male and female. Perhaps, since He made us, He knows how and why He did it as He did. Perhaps, He knows our needs and His plans for all of us, male and female, better than we do. Perhaps, we should trust Him and believe that He wants what is best for us as only He knows our deepest needs.

If you have ever experienced a serious conflict between another couple in your presence, you most likely felt strangely pulled into that conflict. You probably found it easy to take sides and to want to give advice. You might have even become anxious and troubled.

Let me give a personal example to make the point which seems relevant to this question. A number of years ago I was leading a group in a

A SCRIPTURAL GUIDE TO A FULFILLING MARRIAGE

church and my wife was a member of the group. I was talking about the Scriptural teachings concerning Christian marriage and family. I had made a point and someone asked me a question. I do not recall the question but I do recall what happened. Before I could respond, my wife said something like: "Gary has always had problems with that!" She went on to explain how I was wrong and needed to be set straight on that point. I only glared at her I am sure. I was so angry that I never even mentioned the incident to her until years later when the rage came out. It felt so much like the unkind things people had said when I was a child when I questioned what they were teaching me. You see, we had discussed this particular point many times privately and she knew we disagreed and she knew what I believed. She used a public forum to set me straight. I was very humiliated and embarrassed.

Again I would like to point out that there is a linkage in these texts between the behavior of husbands and wives. It is essential to recognize that these instructions are given in tandem. They are linked. There are instructions to wives, then husbands. Sometimes they are reversed, but they are always BOTH THERE. We distort them when we present them any other way.

> "Then we will no longer be infants, tossed back and forth by the waves, and blown here and there by every wind of teaching and by the cunning and crafti-

HUSBANDS, WIVES, WHAT OF THEM?

> ness of men in their deceitful scheming. Instead, speaking the truth in love, we will in all things grow up into him who is the Head, that is, Christ. From him the whole body, joined together by every supporting ligament, grows and builds itself up in love, as each part does its work. ... to be made new in the attitude of your mind; and to put on the new self, created to be like God in true righteousness and holiness." (Ephesians 4: 14-16 and 23, NIV)

Notice the reference to "each part doing its work." God has a plan in the world. He calls each of us, husband and wife, to build each other up in love. He gives different instructions to husbands and wives because He wants us to work together in peace and harmony so that we will bring honor to Him. The metaphors which the Scriptures give illustrate this so beautifully. He wants the world to see Christ in us and be drawn to Him. To reemphasize this point remember the whole passage. Humility stands out repeatedly. Reverence stands out repeatedly. Respect is emphasized over and over again. "She brings him good, not harm, all the days of her life" (Proverbs 31: 12) is the idea in a nutshell.

Social learning theorists say that for a relationship to be stable, there must be equity or distributive justice. I believe that the reason for the different instructions to husbands and wives is

A SCRIPTURAL GUIDE TO A FULFILLING MARRIAGE

because it is necessary to establish a pattern for couples which provides equity and justice between a husband and wife while at the same time providing for a division of labor which enables them to work as a team.

The next passage is found in Colossians 3: 18-19 and it begins with an instruction to wives and it reminds wives that their submission is befitting in the Lord. Wives are to bring honor to Christ.

Husband	Both	Wife
		Wives, submit to your husbands, as is fitting in the Lord.
Husbands, love your wives and do not be harsh with them.		

This particular passage makes the instruction to husbands even more specific. "Do not be harsh with them!" Another reference to abuse. The command is quite direct and clear. The Greek word actually means embitter and this is the only time it is used in the New Testament (Marshall). In Hebrews 12: 14 we read:

> "Make every effort to live in peace with all men and to be holy; without holiness no one will see the Lord. See to it that no one misses the grace of God and that NO BITTER ROOT GROWS up to cause trou-

HUSBANDS, WIVES, WHAT OF THEM?

ble and defile many." (emphasis mine, NIV)

When we do not avail ourselves of the grace of God (self-righteousness), we become bitter and we cause TROUBLE AND DEFILE those around us. By availing ourselves of the grace of God, we recognize our own sinfulness and dependency upon God. This leads us to recognize our own failures and our own need for forgiveness. That enables us to marvel at God's grace toward us and in receiving His love and forgiveness, we reach out to others in love and sympathy.

The next passage is found in Hebrews 13: 4 and it discusses the Scriptural standard for sexual intercourse and the consequences for violating God's law.

Husbands	*Both*	*Wife*
	Marriage should be honored by all, and the marriage bed kept pure, for God will judge the adulterer and all the sexually immoral.	

This statement states very clearly that God wants us to honor marriage. Sexual relationships are reserved for those who are married and extra or pre-marital SEXUAL relationships are sinful and will be judged by God. This emphasis is con-

A SCRIPTURAL GUIDE TO A FULFILLING MARRIAGE

stant throughout the Scriptures. In these permissive days, God's expectations have not changed. The "anything goes" philosophy of our day makes it very, very difficult for the single, separated and divorced people in the Christian community. While Christians cannot change God's standards in this regard, these persons need our love, support and prayers.

The next passage found in I Peter 3: 1-8 discusses the behavior of a wife who is married to an unbeliever.

Husbands	*Both*	*Wife*
		Wives, in the same way be submissive to your husbands so that, if any of them do not believe the word, they may be won over without talk by the behavior of their wives when they see the purity and reverence of your lives. Your beauty should not come from outward adornment, such as braided hair and the wearing of gold jewelry and fine clothes. Instead, it should be that of your INNER SELF, the

HUSBANDS, WIVES, WHAT OF THEM?

Husband	*Both*	*Wife*
		unfading beauty of a GENTLE AND QUIET spirit, which is of great worth in God's sight. For this is the way the holy women of the past who put their hope in God used to make themselves beautiful. They were submissive to their own husbands, like Sarah, who obeyed Abraham and called him her master. You are her daughters if you do what is right and do not give way to fear.
Husbands, in the same way be CONSIDERATE as you live with your wives, and treat them with RESPECT as the weaker partner and as heirs with you of the gracious gift of life, so that nothing will hinder your prayers." (emphasis mine)		

These instructions written by Peter have often been interpreted in very legalistic ways. This instruction becomes a list of things to NOT do. Such an interpretation misses the intent of the admonition. The point is that God's way is different than ours. His way is a quiet and gentle way. Preaching at people, especially loved ones, does not work. It most often turns them off and often they begin to build walls in order to keep your message out. Peter says that an inner beauty of a gentle and quiet spirit is more helpful than outward appearances. He challenges wives to have an inner purity and reverence. Deep respect for their husbands allows God's Holy Spirit to use that inner beauty and reverence to draw them to God. The last phrase is significant. "You are her daughters if you do what is right and do NOT GIVE WAY TO FEAR" (emphasis mine). I believe that the message here is that wives must trust God (not giving away to fear) to use their inner beauty, reverence and respect for God and for their husbands to win their husbands to Him. The Holy Spirit can draw them to Jesus for that is His ministry. This same idea is expressed in I Peter 3: 15:

> "Be ready at any time to give a quiet and reverent answer to any man who wants a reason for the hope that you have within you. Make sure that your conscience is perfectly clear, so that if men should speak slanderously of you as rogues they

HUSBANDS, WIVES, WHAT OF THEM?

> may come to feel ashamed of themselves for libeling your good Christian behavior." (Letters)

God's Holy Spirit can use our lives to win others to God. If we practice what is taught here and throughout the Scriptures (notice that I Peter 3: 15 tells all Christians to do exactly what he tells wives in the passage we are studying), God will draw unbelievers (husbands and others) to Himself.

I previously stated that women were told to be submissive which I have said means that they are to seek peace and harmony and that the word obedience was not used. However, in the second part of the quotation from Hebrews 13:4, we read the implication that wives were to obey their husbands as Sarah did. Oh my, there goes my whole thesis! Or does it? Notice carefully that this verse still says that wives are to be submissive to their husbands and the example given says that Sarah obeyed her husband.

As I prayed about this passage (and frankly even though this is the only time that the word obedience is used, I was troubled by it), I remembered that I have been saying that we must keep things in their context. So I read all of the references to Sarah in the Scriptures. If you wish to read them all, here are the references: Genesis 11: 29-30, 12: 10-17, 16: 1-16, 17: 15-19, 18: 9-15, 20: 2-18, 21: 1-7, 23: 1-2 and 19; Romans 4: 19 and 9: 9; Hebrews 11: 11 and 13: 4. How do the Scriptures record this obedience of Sarah?

A SCRIPTURAL GUIDE TO A FULFILLING MARRIAGE

"Now Sarai, Abram's wife, had borne him no children. But she had an Egyptian maidservant named Hagar; so SHE SAID to Abram, 'The Lord has kept me from having children. GO SLEEP WITH MY MAIDSERVANT; perhaps I can build a family through her.'

Abram AGREED to what Sarai said. So after Abram had been living in Canaan ten years, Sarai his wife TOOK her Egyptian maidservant Hagar and GAVE her to her husband to be his wife. He slept with Hagar, and she conceived.

When she knew she was pregnant, she began to despise her mistress. Then Sarai said to Abram. 'YOU ARE RESPONSIBLE for the wrong I am suffering. I PUT my servant in your arms and now that she knows she is pregnant, she despises me. May the Lord judge between you and me.

'Your servant is in your hands,' Abram said. 'Do with her whatsoever you think best.' Then Sarai mistreated Hagar; and she fled from her." (emphasis mine, Genesis 16: 1-6, NIV)

As I read that passage, I could not ascertain that Sarai (renamed Sarah later) was obeying her husband. In fact, it seems the other way around! Per-

HUSBANDS, WIVES, WHAT OF THEM?

haps, in later stories she changes and then she obeys her husband.

> " 'Where is your wife Sarah?' they asked him. 'There in the tent', he said. Then the Lord said, 'I will surely return to you about this time next year, and Sarah your wife will have a son.' Now Sarah was listening at the entrance to the tent, which was behind him. Abraham and Sarah were already old and well advanced in years, and Sarah was past the age of childbearing. So Sarah laughed to herself as she thought, 'After I am worn out and my master is old, will I now have this pleasure?'
>
> Then the Lord said to Abraham, 'why did Sarah laugh and say, 'Will I really have a child, now that I am old? Is anything too hard for the Lord?' I will return to you at the appointed time next year and Sarah will have a son.'
>
> Sarah was afraid, so she lied and said, 'I did not laugh.' But he said, 'Yes, you did laugh.' " (Genesis 18: 9-15, NIV)

Here we see that Sarah laughed at the promise of God and then she lied. She sounds just like us, doesn't she? No apparent reference to obedience here either.

A SCRIPTURAL GUIDE TO A FULFILLING MARRIAGE

At the conclusion of the record concerning the birth of Isaac we read:

> "Sarah said, 'God has brought me laughter, and everyone who hears about this will laugh with me.' And she added, 'Who would have said to Abraham that Sarah would nurse children? Yet I have borne him a son in his old age.'" (Genesis 21: 6-7, NIV)

I encourage you to read all of the texts. We find the description of two very imperfect human beings whose fears and disobedience stand out quite visibly. God has left that kind of record of most of the great Biblical characters. Since there is no reference to Sarah obeying Abraham, why does Peter say that Sarah obeyed Abraham. Perhaps, Peter knew through inspiration more than we do of the record and that is certainly possible. Yet, it seems that God would show us what He expects of us and give us examples to follow. It may be then, that we are looking for the wrong thing. Maybe, what record is left for us does describe what Peter refers to as obedience. Jesus says that we obey the whole law if we love the Lord our God with our whole being and love our neighbor as ourselves. What I see from this account between Abraham and Sarah is very similar to what I see in all of our relationships today. I believe that this record was left for our learning and Sarah is one of those examples. If she were portrayed as an angel, we

HUSBANDS, WIVES, WHAT OF THEM?

would be overwhelmed by the reality of our own daily lives.

In the final analysis, both Sarah and Abraham did believe God and it was counted to them as righteousness. What I do believe you find very clearly in these passages is that Sarah greatly respected her husband and that God blessed them with a son, the son of the promise long after the age for either of them to have children.

While the words, submission and obedience seem to be used interchangeably by Peter here, he does not use the word obedience when referring to wives. It appears that the idea of respect, reverence and love is overwhelmingly present.

In summary, therefore, I believe that the same idea is presented here in I Peter 3: 1-8 as is presented elsewhere. Husbands are told to be considerate and respectful of their wives. The Greek word used in this passage is interpreted by Marshall as co-heirs when referring to wives. No chain-of-command there! No hierarchy described here either! What is described is a loving, gracious interactional pattern for husbands *and* wives. The wife is to do her husband good and not harm all the days of her life. She is to show him reverence and respect. She is to seek harmony and peace. The husband is to love his wife, to be gentle with her, to be kind and considerate of her needs and he is to be a source of nourishment and blessing.

As I finish this chapter, I am thrilled at God's love and I find that these instructions to couples

A SCRIPTURAL GUIDE TO A FULFILLING MARRIAGE

are beautiful and magnificent. I am also aware of the high responsibility placed on me as a husband. I find that these expectations of me make me aware of my own sinfulness, willfulness, selfishness and my utter dependence upon God to fulfill these expectations. I need His mercy and grace. I fall so short and fail so often. God's standards for me as a husband are so far above me that my own "good works" are never sufficient. I cannot earn His love or grace. They are a free gift. To be this kind of husband I need the guidance and love of Christ and I need to be filled with his Spirit so that the Fruit of the Spirit can become more evident in my daily interactions with my wife.

Sheldon Vanauken expresses a deep respect and love for his wife in this way:

> "In a deep, profound way she recognized that marriage was not a matter of confrontation or competition with her mate, but rather of cooperation. Her remarkable feminine instincts recognized her role as that of complementing her husband. She was fully aware that her magnetic feminine charms and exquisite loveliness, instead of being paraded for personal gratification, could be the great magnet which bound me to her as a man, proud and glad to be her friend and life companion. She rejoiced in being my beloved." (*A Severe Mercy*).

HUSBANDS, WIVES, WHAT OF THEM?

Such a loving and complementary relationship is what I believe the Scriptures describe for believers. What could be more satisfying and full? I have heard many people searching for it in everything and everywhere. One of the reasons it may be so illusive in our day is that we have disgarded what the Scriptures say about the relationship pattern for husbands and wives.

There are sources of professional help for couples unable to work through their conflicts and to find peace and harmony. Chapter six will discuss how persons can find a counselor who both respects their values and faith and is competent to help.

6
Sources of Help

There are presently many different orientations to marital and family therapy. Many different theoretical orientations are used by counselors who are Christians. There are a number of popular books on Christian Counseling and many pastors have training as marriage and family counselors. Many churches and groups with a sectarian sponsorship have begun Christian Counseling programs and some are sponsoring lay counseling programs.

It can be a very confusing world when a couple or family is seeking help with family problems which they have been unable to resolve by themselves. There are times when it is wise for a couple to seek professional help. If you decide to seek professional help, how do you find a counselor who will respect your faith commitments and your value system and who is also competent to help you?

I believe that it is important to recognize that there are many very different meanings to the label, "Christian Counseling". Persons who call themselves Christian counselors vary greatly in terms of competence, Christian commitment, sponsorship, training, orientation to counseling, and methods for helping. These methods vary from very non-directive, non-judgmental approaches to very directive and very judgmental methods.

The Gift of Counseling

I believe that the Scriptures teach that it is the Holy Spirit who gives particular gifts to believers and I believe that counseling is one of those God given gifts. I also believe that it is the Holy Spirit who uses those gifts which He has given to us to bring about healing and reconciliation. I base this claim on Jesus's own words:

> "But I tell you the truth: It is for your good that I am going away. Unless I go away, the COUNSELOR [that is the Holy Spirit] will not come to you: but if I go, I will send him to you. WHEN HE COMES, HE WILL CONVICT THE WORLD OF GUILT IN REGARD TO SIN AND RIGHTEOUSNESS AND JUDGEMENT; in regard to sin, because men do not believe in me; in regard to righteousness, because I am going to the Father, where you will see me no longer; and in regard to judgment, because the

SOURCES OF HELP

> prince of this world now stands condemned." (Emphasis mine, John 16: 7-11, NIV)

So I believe that the Work of the Holy Spirit and the gifts of the Holy Spirit are central to "Christian Counseling". Jesus said that He was sending the Holy Spirit for that very purpose and He calls the Holy Spirit "the Counselor". Paul said:

> "We have different gifts, according to the grace given us. If a man's gift is prophesying, let him use it in proportion to his faith. If it is serving, let him serve; if it is teaching, let him teach; if it is encouraging, let him encourage; if it is contributing to the needs of others, let him give generously; if it is leadership, let him govern diligently; if it is showing mercy, let him do it cheerfully." (Romans 12: 6-8, NIV)

And in I Corinthians 12: 7-11, we read:

> "Now to each one the manisfestation of the Spirit is given for the COMMON GOOD. To one there is given through the Spirit the message of WISDOM, to another the message of KNOWLEDGE by means of the same Spirit, to another FAITH by the same Spirit, to another the

GIFTS OF HEALING by that same Spirit, to another MIRACULOUS POWERS, to another PROPHECY, to another the ability to DISTINGUISH BETWEEN SPIRITS, to another the ability to speak in DIFFERENT KINDS OF TONGUES, and to still another the INTERPRETATION OF TONGUES. All these are the work of one and the same Spirit, and he gives them to each one, JUST AS HE DETERMINES." (emphasis mine, NIV)

I believe that these Scriptures are very clear and I, therefore, conclude that it is essential to recognize that it is the WORK OF THE HOLY SPIRIT IN THE COUNSELOR'S LIFE AND IN THE CLIENT'S LIFE THAT IS CENTRAL TO "CHRISTIAN COUNSELING."

Another emphasis in the Christian Counseling movement is upon the role of "sin" in the counseling process. The place of sin in the evolution of problems is a very complex issue and it is not the subject of this book. However, many "Christian Counselors" emphasize that problems are the result of the client's violation of the principles and practices of the Scriptures. Sometimes the expression "Biblical Behaviors" is used to describe those behaviors which these counselors believe to be expected Christian behaviors.

In contrast to many of these counselors, I believe that the Scriptures teach that it is the work

SOURCES OF HELP

of the Holy Spirit to convict of sin and not the work of a counselor, see John 16: 7-11 above.

When not referring to the specific sins listed as acts of the sinful nature (see page 33), the Scriptures clearly and repeatedly teach us that what might be sin for one person is not necessarily sin for another. For instance, Paul states that when we act apart from faith, we sin!

> "So whatever you believe about these things KEEP BETWEEN YOURSELF AND GOD. Blessed is the man who does not condemn himself by what he approves. But the man who has doubts is condemned if he eats, because his eating is not from faith; and everything THAT DOES NOT COME FROM FAITH IS SIN." (emphasis mine, Romans 14: 22-23, NIV)

Paul clearly states that personal convictions about what is approved is between the individual and God. He clearly states, as Jesus did repeatedly, that a person's motives and intentions are of critical importance.

I, therefore, believe that when a counselor attempts to assume the role of the Holy Spirit in the life of other persons, that is, convicting of sin, or more specifically, determining what sin(s) has created the problem for the client; I believe that the counselor has moved into an inappropriate role. Bruce Narramore says:

> "The Spirit motivates us to holiness by reminding us of our position in Christ and of our freedom from the law and its accompanying condemnation." *(No Condemnation Rethinking Guilt Motivation in Counseling, Preaching, & Parenting*, page 174)

Our position in Jesus Christ is not sin focused, it is Christ focused. I believe that the same obviously applies to "Christian Counseling".

> "Since you died with Christ to the basic principles of this world, why, as though you still belonged to it, do you submit to its rules: Do not handle! Do not taste! Do not touch!
>
> These are all destined to perish with use, because they are based on HUMAN commands and teachings. Such regulations indeed have an appearance of wisdom, with their self-imposed worship, their false humility and their harsh treatment of the body, but they lack any value in restraining sensual indulgence." (emphasis mine, Colossians 2: 20-23, NIV)

SOURCES OF HELP

Narramore states:

> "Here we have a legalistic, performance-based style of morality that at first glance, appears to be the precise opposite of an impulsive, lustful style of morality. When viewed from another perspective, however, these two orientations can be seen to have a great deal in common. They are actually alternative ways of expressing the same fleshly (sin) principle." (Ibid, page 173)

Narramore goes on to say (page 174-5) that the legalistic expression of the flesh says:

> "I am the authority regarding criteria of spirituality; I will define it as conformity to certain standards."

Actually, it seems as though Paul is equating *legalism* with *humanism* as is seen in the text above (Colossians 2: 20-22). It has been my observation through the years, that a focus upon sin (or "biblical behaviors") almost always degenerates into a conformity model of Christianity and, therefore, I believe that when a counselor begins to focus upon sin, the counselor can very quickly move into a legalistic, conformity model of encouraging people to move back into spiritual bondage.

A SCRIPTURAL GUIDE TO A FULFILLING MARRIAGE

Futhermore, I believe that when a counselor begins to confront clients with their sin, the counselor cannot help but move into a judgmental stance and the counselor cannot help but function from the counselor's own perception of what the sin problem is. I believe that such a stance almost always alienates and puts people on the defensive. It seldom brings about healing or reconciliation. When the counselor moves into confronting a client with sin, the counselor becomes the decider of which sin is creating the problem for the client. I believe it is the work of the Holy Spirit alone because a counselor cannot possibly know the will of God for another person nor can the counselor know what the sin problem is for another person (some Scriptural exceptions to this will be discussed in the following pages).

> "And in the same way—by our faith—the Holy Spirit helps us with our daily problems and in our praying. We don't EVEN KNOW WHAT WE SHOULD PRAY FOR NOR HOW TO PRAY as we should; but the Holy Spirit prays for us with such feeling that it cannot be expressed in words. And the Father who knows all hearts knows, of course, what the Spirit is saying as he pleads for us in HARMONY WITH GOD'S OWN WILL" (emphasis mine, Romans 8: 26-27, Living)

Whenever a Christian counselor assumes the work of the Holy Spirit, the counselor almost al-

SOURCES OF HELP

ways must judge from outward appearances. That is, the counselor can only operate on the basis of what has been said in the counselor's presence (which often neglects the historical reasons for what the counselor may be seeing at this point in time). Furthermore, the counselors can only operate on their own biases about what "Biblical Behaviors" are (do they include dancing, smoking, movies, television, etc.?). The counselors, as other imperfect human beings, will often project what their own motives might be in that circumstance. Jesus said:

> "For out of the heart come evil thoughts, murder, adultery, sexual immorality, theft, false testimony, slander. These are what make a man 'unclean'; but eating with unwashed hands does not make him 'unclean.'" (Matthew 15,19-20, NIV)

> "You have heard that it was said, 'Do not commit adultery.' But I tell you that anyone who looks at a woman lustfully has already committed adultery in his heart." (Matthew 5:28, NIV)

The point that I am trying to make is that a counselor cannot know the inner motives and thoughts of a client. The client may also be purposively deceiving the counselor and the counselor may have no awareness of that deception. I recently counseled with a husband who had been extremely abusive of his wife for many years and to hear his account you would think he was absolutely faultless. Furthermore, because of defense mechanisms such as repression, the clients frequently are not consciously aware of their own motives. It is essential to also remember that motivation is almost always very complex.

I have so often come to understand after many hours of counseling that my initial perceptions were based on a false picture of the real situation. For instance, in abusive situations, I have often come to understand why the abused person refuses to consider reconciliation. That abusing person has most often been forgiven many times and that forgiveness has only led to more and more abuse.

The only appropriate and, I believe, Scriptural response to abuse is separation from the abusing person until there is TRUE and GENUINE repentance (which means that a basic change has occurred and that the abuse has and will remain stopped). I have also learned that such abusive situations over time often destroy any remaining love and respect and that reconciliation is not humanly possible.

I might add here that the danger of becoming part of the problem rather than becoming a healing force in the life of the client is not unique to the Christian counselor. However, I believe that there is a far greater danger when the problem is confounded by calling it Christian. The claim that one is a Christian Counselor increases the respon-

SOURCES OF HELP

sibility to be helpful rather than hurtful and to bring about healing rather than further alienation. It may also create the possibility that the counseling process not only alienates the person from seeking further counseling but may also alienate them from the Good News of God's loving kindness toward them.

It is important to remember that counselors are human beings and they, themselves, are at all levels of emotional and spiritual growth. Their helpfulness is also very directly related to the gifts that God has given to them. They can become legalistic and rigid. They often fail to recognize their own sinfulness and fallibility.

I believe that it is also important to understand that many persons who call themselves Christian counselors have very limited knowledge of the Scriptures and some of them have very little professional training. Counselors are also people with varied levels of mental health, themselves.

It would also seem apparent to me that counselors are often insensitive to the total life experiences of the people involved and, therefore, are quite capable of making very bad miscalculations about which sinful or unbiblical behaviors to focus upon. Furthermore, I believe that this whole process (confronting sin) is not up to counselors (See below the discussion about the responsibility of spiritual leaders to deal with certain specific sinful patterns of behavior). When a counselor or other Christian attempts to assume the Holy

A SCRIPTURAL GUIDE TO A FULFILLING MARRIAGE

Spirit's work in the life of another Christian, I believe that they are violating a far more essential principle of the Scriptures: "Do Not Judge".

God has brought many persons to me for counseling through the years who were extremely angry and hurt by the responses of other Christians to their life circumstances; such as divorce, abuse and emotional problems. It has seemed to me that often the only helpful thing I could do was to provide an atmosphere of love and understanding absolutely free of judgment or condemnation.

Another closely related issue is that of using prayer in client-counselor sessions. Many of the experiences in relation to both the use and misuse of prayer that I had as a child, were so hurtful that for years I had difficulty accepting prayer as much more than a hostile manipulation of my perceptions and feelings.

Often when our family would be in the midst of conflict and tension and when I was so angry that I could hardly control myself, I would be forced to pray for dinner, etc. I resented that use of prayer and, yet, I could not share that thought and feeling because of the fear that not only would I anger my father but I might also anger God. While I do not know my father's motivation, I do know its effect upon me.

I also experienced people praying fancy prayers in church who reminded me of the parable of Jesus about the self-righteous person praying in the synagogue (Luke 18: 10-11). One of those per-

SOURCES OF HELP

sons was so hateful and argumentative that I thought he was certainly the greatest hypocrite I had ever met.

I also experienced people praying at me during their prayers or using prayer as a way to lecture me. This, of course, made any response impossible because I was certainly not going to interrupt someone who was praying.

I use this personal example to demonstrate how foolish it is to attempt to develop any generalizations about the use of prayer in the counseling situation. Such generalizations can become a simple routine and lose any of its intended purpose.

I recall that at Wheaton College, prayer before class often seemed that way and in a lot of classes it lost any meaning at all. I must add, however, that one man's prayers and devotions never seemed that way and, in fact, I loved to hear him pray and I looked forward to his devotional times.

I believe that "Christian Counselors" (I would much rather say counselors who are Christians) must be especially sensitive to the client's feelings and perceptions in these regards because they are often viewed as representing the Christian faith as well as the counseling profession to which they belong.

God has given different abilities to each of us and His gifts to us are the most effective means for us to serve Him. Those gifts are the medium He uses. Sometimes the only approach is careful listening and loving. At other times, confrontation (not judgment) is the most effective means of reaching a person. There are few rules and regulations that always apply. There are gifts and when all else has failed, there is love.

Another issue in "Christian Counseling" is that of competence. I am alarmed at much of the present movement within churches to train lay people to be counselors. The idea that all one has to do is to be a "born again Christian" to be a competent counselor is not only dangerous, it is terribly erroneous from a Scriptural point of view:

> "There are different kinds of gifts, but the same Spirit. There are many different kinds of service, but the same Lord. There are many different kinds of working, but the same God works all of them in all men.
>
> Now to each one the manifestation of the Spirit is given for the COMMON GOOD. To one there is given through the Spirit the message of WISDOM, to another the message of KNOWLEDGE by means of the same Spirit, to another FAITH by the same Spirit, to another the gifts of HEALING by that one Spirit, to another MIRACULOUS POWERS, to another PROPHECY, to another the ability to DISTINGUISH between spirits, to another the ability to SPEAK in different

SOURCES OF HELP

> kinds of tongues, and still another the INTERPRETATION of tongues. All these are the work of one and the same Spirit, and he gives them to each one, JUST AS HE DETERMINES" (emphasis mine, I Corinthians 12:4-11, NIV).

This emphasis is constant throughout the Bible. A beautiful description of this idea is found in Exodus 35: 30-36:

> "See, the Lord has chosen Bezalel, son of Uri, ... and has filled him with the Spirit of God, with skill, ability and knowledge in all kinds of crafts—(NIV).

The central idea expressed over and over again is that the Holy Spirit both gives us our gifts and is responsible for the outcome in the lives of others as we minister through the use of our gifts.

Many clients have come to see me and expressed great dismay and hurt over the counsel that had been given them by untrained, inexperienced, church supported, lay counselors. Many of these people went to these counselors at times of great turmoil in their lives. These persons have reported that the advice they received was often so ill-advised that it created and/or maintained abusive environments for those Christians, many of whom were new Christians. Another frequent area of bad counsel has been around the whole issue of anger in the life of a believer.

A SCRIPTURAL GUIDE TO A FULFILLING MARRIAGE

The Pauline Epistles have a great deal to say about the role of the church in ministering to its people. The major emphasis in the Scriptures is always upon the ministry of agape love. After Paul refers to all of the gifts of the Spirit, he says

> "But eagerly desire the greater gifts. And now I will show you the most excellent way.
>
> If I speak in the tongues of men and of angels, but have not love, I am only a resounding gong or a clanging cymbal.
>
> If I have the gift of prophecy and can fathom all mysteries and all knowledge, and if I have a faith that can move mountains, but have not love, I am nothing.
>
> If I give all I possess to the poor and surrender my body to the flames, but have not love, I gain nothing.
>
> Love is patient,
> Love is kind.
>
> It does not envy, it does not boast, it is not proud.
>
> It is not rude,
> It is not self-seeking,
> it is not easily angered,
> it keeps no record of wrongs.

SOURCES OF HELP

> Love does not delight in evil but rejoices in the truth.
>
> It always protects,
> always trusts,
> always hopes,
> always perseveres.
> LOVE NEVER FAILS." (emphasis mine, I Corinthians 13: 1-8, NIV)

Some years ago I had an experience that I shall never forget. I worked for a religious agency as a social worker. We had devotions once a week as a staff. One day when it was my turn, I used the above text and I really gave it to them. I left the room feeling very smug and with a feeling of superiority. In the entrance way there was a large mural of Jesus and I remember looking at the picture as I was walking through the entrance way. I, then, recall that I thought someone touched me on the shoulder and said: "What about you, Gary?" I turned around startled and no one was there. I was so devastated that it took me some time to regain my composure. I could only sit in my office absolutely stunned.

Hurting people need a sense of community which is supportive and loving. This is the constant emphasis upon the ministry of the body of Christ. So often we replace love with everything else and convince ourselves that we are ministering effectively.

When it comes to sin in the life of the believer, the Scriptures are quite clear about the role of the "body of believers" and the definition of sin. Consider:

> "Brothers, if someone is caught in a sin, you who are SPIRITUAL should restore him GENTLY. But watch yourself, or you also may be tempted. Carry each other's burden, and in this way you will fulfill the law of Christ. If anyone thinks he is something when he is nothing, he deceives himself. Each one should test his own actions. Then he can take pride in himself, without comparing himself to somebody else, for each one should carry his own load. ... Therefore, as we have opportunity, let us do good to all people, especially to those who belong to the family of believers." (emphasis mine, Galatians 6: 1-10, NIV)

It is critical to note that those who are SPIRITUAL should gently restore the person caught in sin. Being SPIRITUAL is the first consideration in who goes to the person caught in sin (whether that person is a counselor is incidental to whether or not the counselor is spiritual). What do the Scriptures mean when they say that those who are spiritual should gently restore?

> "But the fruit of the Spirit is love, joy, peace, patience, kindness, goodness, faithfulness, gentleness and self-control." (Galatians 5:22, NIV)

SOURCES OF HELP

Here we see that the focus for a person who is Spiritual is not on behaviors (do and do not) per se but upon the fruit of the Spirit.

What is Paul referring to as "caught in sin"?

> "The acts of the sinful nature are obvious: sexual immorality, IMPURITY, and debauchery; idolatry and witchcraft: HATRED, DISCORD, JEALOUSY, FITS OF RAGE, SELFISH AMBITION, DISSENSIONS, FACTIONS AND ENVY; drunkenness, orgies, and the like." (emphasis mine, Galatians 5:19-21, NIV)

Wow! How about that list? Do you consider yourself spiritual in light of these sins? No wonder the instruction includes the caution about being careful that the spiritual ones might also be tempted, themselves. I believe that it is essential to understand how very frail we are when it comes to God's standards. No wonder Jesus said that He is the Vine and we are the branches and that without Him, we can do nothing.

It appears to me, therefore, that Christian Counseling's first criteria is that counselors must be persons who clearly and consistently demonstrate the fruit of the Spirit in their own lives, who have the gifts necessary for counseling and who understand their own dependency upon God's grace, first for themselves, and then for those they are counseling. In order to be spiritual (not in the legalistic way of not doing certain things, etc.), one must recognize his own sinfulness. He must recognize that "there but for the grace of God, go I!"

I love to read over and over again the Good News. Jesus was so different! His loving interactions with sinners never fail to move me. You see, I am a sinner! I sin more often and more repeatedly than I am willing to admit to anyone but God, and to Him only because I know He already knows. That is why Paul warns us to be watchful. It is easy to "not touch, not eat or drink and not to do certain things". It is far more difficult to "live out the fruit of the Spirit"! And, in fact, we cannot live out the fruit of the Spirit, only He can do that through us!

> "And this is my prayer; that your love may abound more and more in knowledge and depth of insight, so that you may be able to discern what is best and may be pure and blameless until the day of Christ, filled with the fruit of righteousness that comes through Jesus Christ—to the glory and praise of God." (Philippians 1: 9-11, NIV)

The point that I am trying to make is quite simple in reality. I am only a vessel! You are only a vessel! We are the clay, He is the Potter!

A person is a "Christian" Counselor only to the degree that the Holy Spirit can use the gifts that He has given to them. It is His work! He has given us gifts. And He will use those gifts to the common good.

SOURCES OF HELP

If you have one gift and I have another and you want mine or I want yours, then we are guilty of at least one of the sins listed in the passage above: selfish ambition, jealousy, or envy.

While there are obviously ministries for each person within the Body of Christ, these must be within the gifts that God has given each of us. So often I have seen evidence that a great deal of damage is being done by lay counseling programs and, in general, I believe that there are inadequate safeguards in the preparation, training and selection process. I encourage my readers to be very careful in choosing a counselor.

> "Let no debt remain outstanding, except the continuing debt to love one another, for he who loves his fellow man has fulfilled the law. The commandments, 'Do not commit adultery,' 'Do not murder,' 'Do not covet,' and whatever commandment there may be, are summed up in this one rule: 'Love your neighbor as yourself.' Love does no harm to its neighbor. Therefore love is the fulfillment of the law." (Romans 13: 8-19, NIV)

God's law of love is given to us to bring us inner peace and joy rather than outward appearances. God's plans for our relationships are holy and beautiful. God's plans for us provide equity and love.

A SCRIPTURAL GUIDE TO A FULFILLING MARRIAGE

Healing through Counseling

In his book, *Helping Couples Change* (Ibid, page 27), Richard Stuart states:

> "The same principle is fundamental to all attempts to promote change in marital and family behavior. Distressed family members often complain that their feelings of love for others have died. They plaintively ask therapists to help restore those treasured feelings before they begin, anew, loving behaviors toward their mates. But the feelings of love can grow only through interaction with the other; therefore, the key to relationship change is that the love-lost client must act toward the other as if loving feelings were alive and well, for only then will the other's loving actions be stimulated—actions that can truly support our client's love for his or her mate. Therapeutic behavior change of every sort is therefore seen to depend upon the therapist's skills in encouraging the client's willingness to reach beyond reality and to summon the willingness to act AS IF the world were a welcoming place, for it must remain the forbidding place it is believed to be until these behaviors occur."

I believe that the Scriptures teach us this same principle. Only as believers act AS IF the

SOURCES OF HELP

other person loves them and acts in loving ways, themselves, can they begin to see the power of love. Love most often creates love. As a counselor, I often see couples who are into vengeance and retaliation. They are keeping score and they feel compelled to pay each other back for real or imagined wrongs. The Scriptures say:

> "Finally, all of you, live in harmony with one another, be sympathetic, love as brothers, be compassionate and humble. Do not repay evil with evil or insult with insult, but with blessing. For, 'Whoever would love life and see good days must keep his tongue from evil and his lips from deceitful speech. He must turn from evil and do good; he must seek peace and pursue it. For the eyes of the Lord are on the righteous and his ears are attentive to their prayer, but the face of the Lord is against those who do evil." (I Peter 3: 8-12, NIV)

Many of the approaches to curbing divided homes today within the leadership of many churches remind me of Nehemiah as recorded in Nehemiah 13: 25:

> "I rebuked them and called curses down on them. I beat some of the men and pulled out their hair. I made them take an oath in God's name and said: 'You are not to give your daughters in marriage to

their sons, nor are you to take their daughters in marriage for your sons or yourselves. (NIV)

In Deuteronomy we read the following instruction:

> "When you go to war against your enemies and the Lord your God delivers them into your hands and you take captives, if you notice a beautiful woman and are attracted to her, you may take her as your wife. Bring her into your home and have her shave her head, trim her nails and put aside the clothes she was wearing when captured. After she has lived in your house and mourned her father and mother for a full month, then you may go to her and be her husband and she shall be your wife. If you are not pleased with her, let her go wherever she wishes. You must not sell her or treat her as a slave, since you have dishonored her." (Deuteronomy 20: 19-20, NIV)

Also compare this with God's message to Zechariah in Zechariah 7: 8-9:

> "This is what the Lord Almighty says: 'Administer justice; show mercy and compassion to one another. Do not oppress the widow or the fatherless, the alien or

SOURCES OF HELP

> the poor. In your hearts do not think evil
> of each other.' " (NIV)

God's way is a way of love, of justice, of mercy, and of peace. His way is a way of service. His way is a way of holiness and purity. His way is a way of harmony and joy. Christian counseling must then certainly be loving and compassionate!

The standard that God has set for His children, believers, is love and holiness. Since God is love and holy, we must walk in obedience to Him if He is to bless us. Moreover, whenever we take over the work of the Holy Spirit in the lives of others, we become instant failures. We often become judgmental, hostile and pushy and we often substitute outward appearances for inner purity. While Nehemiah wanted to purify his people and bring them back to God, he tried to force his will upon them. His methods were unfair and abusive. He actually forced people to divorce their wives. Jesus points out that sin comes from the heart and not from those around us.

Look at the contrast between Nehemiah's methods and those which Peter gave to the believers who were married to unbelievers—quiet, reverent love (I Peter 3: 1-6). We often resort to Nehemiah's methods and drive our loved ones away from us and away from God. Force leads to rebellion and/or conformity. It does not lead to obedience.

A SCRIPTURAL GUIDE TO A FULFILLING MARRIAGE

God leads us to genuine change rather than conformity. Our hearts and lives are to become more and more like Jesus. Our behavior toward ourselves, our mates, our children, our fellow believers is to be loving, peaceful, considerate, respectful and non-argumentative.

Bruce Narramore states:

"To avoid potentially debilitating guilt, some individuals under sway of such needless inhibitions carefully structure their lives according to a series of do's and don'ts. By rigidly carrying out 'desirable' behaviors and avoiding 'undesirable' ones, they attempt to maintain a sense of fidelity to God and avoid guilt feelings." (*No Condemnation*, page 197)

The emphasis upon Scriptural behaviors, equated with Christian counseling by many authors, frequently drives persons into a copycat, legalistic, conformity model. It most frequently inhibits spiritual growth because the emphasis moves away from one of yielding to the work of the Holy Spirit in one's life to an emphasis upon sin and "right behavior". I strongly recommend Narramore's book, *No Condemnation*, for my readers who wish to explore this issue in more depth.

I have repeatedly stated that I believe that God meets us where we are, rather than where we should be, and begins His work in our hearts and

SOURCES OF HELP

lives from the INSIDE OUT rather than the other way around. The Holy Spirit uses the Scriptures and our own daily life experiences to help us understand and walk in the will of God.

> "All Scripture is God-breathed and is useful for teaching, rebuking, correcting and training in righteousness, so that the man of God may be thoroughly equipped for every good work." (II Timothy 3: 16-17, NIV)

It is important to understand that this Scriptural passage states that the Scriptures, themselves, not other Christians, are responsible for correcting, teaching, rebuking and training us. So often other Christians seem to believe that they are to rebuke, correct and train; and that is not what this passage teaches us at all.

> "For the word of God is living and active. Sharper than any double-edged sword, it PENETRATES even to dividing soul and spirit, joints and marrow, it JUDGES the thoughts and attitudes of the heart. NOTHING IN ALL GOD'S CREATION IS HIDDEN FROM GOD'S SIGHT. Everything is uncovered and laid bare before the eyes of him to whom we must give account. Therefore, since we have a great high priest who has gone through the heavens, Jesus the Son of God, let us

A SCRIPTURAL GUIDE TO A FULFILLING MARRIAGE

> hold firmly to the FAITH we profess. For we do not have a high priest who is unable to sympathize with our weaknesses, but we have one who has been tempted in every way, just as we are—yet without sin. Let us approach the throne of GRACE with CONFIDENCE, so that we many receive MERCY and find GRACE to help us in our time of need." (emphasis mine, Hebrews 4: 12-16, NIV)

Our communication with God is forever relevant to our own individual stage of personal and spiritual growth. The Scriptures teach us that even our faith is a gift of God. Our task is to yield to God's Holy Spirit who lives in us. God gives us the faith we need as we need it and as we yield to the promptings of the Holy Spirit.

It is always personal, it is unique to us, it is different for each one of us and it is always exactly what we need at the moment. So often we try to put God in a box and prescribe how He works. He is far greater than we even begin to imagine. He is infinite! The Christian life is a walk of faith based upon the promises of God. God gives us the faith as we step out in faith.

The Holy Spirit is our link to God. While He speaks to us through our fellowship with other believers, He never turns over to them His work in our lives. The Holy Spirit speaks to us through our prayers, the Scriptures and our daily experiences. He always speaks to us in ways as indivi

SOURCES OF HELP

ual as we are. Healing comes about through grace. We are forgiven because of God's grace alone. Jesus took our punishment and He offers us healing and peace.

What about Forgiveness?

I am convinced that the Scriptures teach that when we repent, are truly sorry for our sins (Narramore calls this Godly sorrow) and make things right with those we have sinned against; that God not only forgives us for our sins but that He restores us to full fellowship.

As I grew up and particularly when I was a student at Prairie Bible Institute, I was taught that I could make some fatal step of disobedience and be out of the will of God for the rest of my life. I must add, however, that L. E. Maxwell, the president of PBI, was one of those persons in my life who demonstrated such love and compassion toward me that his love and understanding helped me over times of fear and doubt. The pain, the hopelessness, the fear, the bondage, the strivings and the eventual loss of hope which led me very close to suicide at the age of twenty-one cannot be adequately portrayed. God's love was there and He broke through to me in a very odd way. I was a student at the Grand Rapids School of the Bible and Music and I was assigned to go to a Gospel Mission to hand out pamphlets (something I hated with a passion). God used a message at that

A SCRIPTURAL GUIDE TO A FULFILLING MARRIAGE

gospel mission (to which I will refer shortly) to show me that He loved me and He began that night so many years ago to deliver me from inhibiting guilt, condemnation and false teaching.

God is still completing that liberating work in my life. The Holy Spirit is still teaching me that God is in the healing business. I am referring to the most basic healing in the universe. Healing the relationship of separation from God and from each other. One of the Scriptures which clearly point to the freedom from past sin and disobedience and to God's ability to restore us to full fellowship is found in a parable of Jesus:

> "For the kingdom of heaven is like a landowner who went out early in the morning to hire men to work in his vineyard. He agreed to pay them a denarius for the day and sent them into his vineyard. About the third hour he went out and saw others standing in the marketplace doing nothing. He told them, 'you also go and work in my vineyard, and I will pay you whatever is right.' So they went. He went out again about the sixth hour and the ninth hour and did the same thing. About the eleventh hour he went out and found still others standing around. He asked them, 'Why have you been standing here all day long doing nothing?' 'Because no one has hired us,' they answered. He said to them, 'You

SOURCES OF HELP

> also go and work in my vineyard.' When evening came, the owner of the vineyard said to his foreman, 'Call the workers and pay them their wages, beginning with the last ones hired and going to the first.' The workers who were hired about the eleventh hour came and each received a denarious. So when those came who were hired first, they expected to receive more. But each one of them also received a denarius. When they received it, they began to grumble against the landowner. 'These men who were hired last worked only one hour,' they said, 'and you have made them equal to us who have borne the burden of the work and the heat of the day.' 'But he answered one of them, 'Friend, I am not being unfair to you. Didn't you agree to work for a denarius? Take your pay and go. I want to give the man who was hired last the same as I gave you. Don't I have the right to do what I want with my own money? Or are you envious because I am generous?' 'So the last will be first, and the first will be last.' " (Matthew 20: 1-16. NIV)

Regardless of when we yield our lives, our wills, our ambitions, our marriages, our families, **HE MEETS US THERE!** He can restore us to His

BEST for us! Love keeps no score of wrongs. God does not deal with us as we tend to deal with each other. When, whenever, we yield ourselves to God, He uses all of our life experiences, our sins as well as our service and our talents to PERFECT THAT WHICH HE HAS BEGUN IN US.

The Scriptures are full of examples of sinful persons who were used of God. If God waited until we were perfect, He could not ever use any of us until we were dead and with Him. We would not have the 51st Psalm if David had not sinned so greviously with Bathsheba and ordered her husband killed to cover his own sin. God uses even our sins to teach us the result of sin in our lives.

Have you ever marvelled at the tremendous change you have seen in a person born of God. God takes our filthy rags and creates a clean heart within us. God's ways are so far above ours. We so often become bound up in good works, rules and regulations, and in distorted perceptions of equality and fairness. He loves us with an unending love and He provides healing when we come to Him and yield our lives to Him.

I believe that too often we want only instant solutions rather than the miracle of healing. God uses our own life experiences to help us grow and to find healing. Even natural healing takes time. Watch a wound heal or an illness heal. God's ways are often very natural and uneventful. Often that process is very slow and even unrecognized. But it is happening! As a counselor, I see that healing occur over and over again.

SOURCES OF HELP

Discernment in the Scriptures

In order to make this point more clear, I will refer to a parable of Jesus. Some years ago I listened to a message in a Gospel Mission in Grand Rapids, Michigan. I do not know the name of the speaker so I cannot credit him for pointing out some of the following observations about Luke 15. As a rebelling and very hurt young person at that point in my life, I found his message very poignant and God used it in my life at the time in a very powerful way. Seeing the infinite love of God and recognizing how Jesus dealt with others, helped me over a time in my life when I felt helpless and overcome with condemnation, guilt, failure and anger. I have never forgotten the message of hope and love it provided.

> "Wouldn't any man among you who owned a hundred sheep, and lost one of them, leave the ninety-nine to themselves in the open, and go after the one which is lost until he finds it? And when he has found it, he will lift it on to his shoulders with great joy, and as soon as he gets home, he will call his friends and neighbors together. 'Rejoice with me,' he will say, 'for I have found that sheep of mine which was lost.' I tell you that it is the same in Heaven—there is more joy over one sinner whose heart is changed than over ninety-nine righteous people

A SCRIPTURAL GUIDE TO A FULFILLING MARRIAGE

> who have no need of repentance." (Luke 15: 4-7, *The New Testament*)

Here Jesus tells us that God's personal concern over one lost person is very significant. The illustration here described by Jesus is that of a sheep. The sheep wanders off and is lost from the flock. This is not the rebellious person who insists upon his own way nor is it the person who has been abused by another person. Sheep just wander off! Many children and adolescents are like that. They do not wilfully or rebelliously leave. They just wander off perhaps looking for better things or more interesting times. Jesus says that the father would seek after that person UNTIL he finds him. He leaves the flock in a safe place and he seeks after the one who has wandered off. If that has happened to your child or mate, the illustration here teaches us to seek after and to search for that person IN LOVE until we find him or her. Then have a celebration! There is joy, not lectures and condemnation; and there is an invitation for others to join in the celebration.

> "... Or if a women who has ten silver coins should lose one, won't she take a lamp and sweep and search the house from top to bottom until she finds it? And when she has found it, she calls her friends and neighbors together. 'Rejoice with me' she says, 'for I have found that coin I lost.' I tell you, it is the same in Heaven—there is rejoicing among the an-

SOURCES OF HELP

> gels of God over one sinner whose heart is changed." (Luke 15: 8-10, New Testament)

In this illustration, Jesus describes the lost coin. In this illustration, the women LOST the coin. The coin did not rebel or wander off, she lost it. The instruction in this case is to TAKE A LAMP, SWEEP AND SEARCH THE HOUSE from TOP to BOTTOM! In this illustration the picture is of a person who has done something harmful or careless to someone else. I believe a coin is used to show clearly that the problem lies with the person who has offended rather than with the recipient of that action. Abuse being one such situation. The erring person is told to clean up his own life from top to bottom. The action requires illumination and diligence. The person who was careless or thoughtless repents and finds what was lost. The solution in this circumstance is to do something with oneself not something to the "coin". Owning one's personal responsibility for the problem was the beginning of the healing process. The next step is to remove the "mess" or "sin" in one's own life. There is rejoicing when the careless or sinful person repents and finds what they have lost.

> "Then he continued: 'Once there was a man who had two sons. The younger one said to his father, 'Father, give me my share of the property that will come to me.' So he divided up his estate between

A SCRIPTURAL GUIDE TO A FULFILLING MARRIAGE

the two of them. Before very long, the younger son collected all his belongings and went off to a distant land, where he squandered his wealth in the wildest extravagance. And when he had run through all his money, a terrible famine arose in that country, and he began to feel the pinch. Then he went and hired himself out to one of the citizens of that country who sent him out into the fields to feed pigs. He got to the point of longing to stuff himself with the food the pigs were eating, and not a soul gave him anything. Then HE CAME TO HIS SENSES and cried aloud, 'Why dozens of my father's hired men have more food than they can eat, and here I am dying of hunger! I will get up and go back to my father, and I will say to him: "Father, I have done wrong in the sight of Heaven and in your eyes. Please take me as one of your hired men.'" So he got up and went to his father. But while he was still some distance off, his father saw him and his heart went out to him, and he ran and fell on his neck and kissed him. But his son said: 'Father, I have done wrong in the sight of Heaven and in your eyes. I don't deserve to be called your son any more...' 'Hurry!' called his father to the servants, 'fetch the best clothes and put them on him! Put a ring on his finger and shoes on his feet, and get the fatted

SOURCES OF HELP

> calf and kill it, we will have a feast and a celebration! For this is my son—he was dead, and he's alive again. He was lost, and he's found!' And they began to get the festivities going." (emphasis mine, Luke 15: 11-24, The New Testament)

The response for the rebellious person was to give him his belongings and let him go. However, the father is watchful and eagerly waiting for his son's return. The rebellious person is not chased, threatened or coerced. He is allowed to learn through his own experiences, he is allowed to go hungry until HE COMES TO HIS SENSES and he is allowed to repent. Then there is forgiveness and restoration and JOY!

> "But his elder son was out in the fields, and as he came near the house, he heard music and dancing. So he called one of the servants across to him and inquired what was the meaning of it all. 'Your brother has arrived, and your father has killed the fatted calf because he has got him home again safe and sound,' was the reply. But he was furious and refused to go inside the house. So his father came outside and and pleaded with him. Then he burst out! 'Look, how many years have I slaved for you and never disobeyed a single order of yours, and yet you have never given me so much as a young goat, so that I could give my friends a dinner!

> But when this son of yours arrives, who has spent all your money on prostitutes, for him you kill the fatted calf!' But the father replied: 'My dear son, you have been with me all the time and everything I have is yours. But we had to celebrate and show our joy. For this is your brother; I thought he was dead—and he's alive. He was lost—and now he is found!' " (Luke 15: 25-32, The New Testament)

The response to the resentful, faithful person is that the father reminds him of his status (all I have is yours) and he reminds him that he has had the benefit of being with the father at all times (fellowship). He reminds him that "we" must be joyful when others repent and come home!

Jesus describes four different reasons for alienation—wandering off, being hurt by another person, being rebellious and being resentful of others who repent and are forgiven. I believe that this is one of the best illustrations of "Christian Counseling" in the Scriptures. Jesus talks about the reasons for alienation and he suggests the way to respond. In order to know how to approach the person who is separated or alienated from us or from God, we must know the reason for that alienation. Is it because of the person's own actions, the actions of others, or is it an unforgiv-

SOURCES OF HELP

ing and resentful attitude. In terms of counseling, the Holy Spirit promises to give us the very wisdom of God and we are promised the ability to be discerning. The elder brother teaches us the result of having a "better-than-thou" attitude and that is that our fellowship and joy are interrupted. The Holy Spirit will aid us in knowing how to approach others, if we seek His guidance and believe His promises. He will also give us the strength, the ability, the fortitude and the love to use the correct approach to others.

Notice that not one of the erring persons was in the right. Neither the wandering person, the person who caused harm to someone else, the person who insisted on his own way and his own pleasure nor the self-righteous person, was in a correct relationship to the father. Each and everyone of them was in a state of separation or alienation. For each, however, the reason for separation was different.

The OVERWHELMING message about the father was his LOVE. There was always joy (not condemnation or vengeance) when there was a reconnection! The father's love was constant and he was always ready to forgive and welcome that person back into fellowship. A message of HOPE!

What was different in each situation was the problem solving approach to the person who was separated. The father's response was different. The lesson taught here by Jesus is one of love, perseverance, patience, compassion, precise timing, watchfulness and honesty.

Are you frozen into a pattern of reacting to others? Do you ask the Holy Spirit to give you guidance and discernment in situations in your life? The Holy Spirit will use the Scriptures, your own prayers, the prayers of others, and your own life experiences to teach you. The only condition we must meet is to be willing to seek and to do His will.

As a counselor, I spend a lot of time helping individuals, couples and families assess the reasons for alienation. While there is no merit or usefulness in affixing blame in the process, it is essential to know why the alienation came about so that the persons involved can know how to find resolution to the difficulty.

I also want to help each person assume responsibility for his or her own contribution to the problem. I believe that the Bible teaches us that each one of us bears responsibilities for our own contribution to the problem regardless of what the other person has or is doing. I make an effort to listen very carefully and to teach the individuals to listen carefully. As people listen carefully to the other person and how they have affected the other person, they can begin to assume responsibility for themselves and to either change the offending behaviors or to help the other person understand why they are acting in those ways. Often this process leads to understanding and forgiveness because both people feel heard and understood. If the cleared up understandings only clarify differences, I use the Relationship En-

SOURCES OF HELP

hancement counseling method to help both persons find a mutually satisfactory resolution. This method is described by Bernard Guerney in his book, *Relationship Enhancement: Skill Training Programs for Therapy, Problem Prevention and Enrichment.*

The skills taught in this program are referred to as: expressive skill, empathic skill, discussion-negotiation skill, problem solving skill, self-change skill, helping-others change skill, generalization skill, teaching skill and maintenance skill. This program is based upon several underlying assumptions which I believe are totally consistent with the teachings of the Scriptures.

Guerney states: "But it is the client who should choose which goals he will try to achieve—what kind of a person he will try to become." (page 9) "The fundamental goal of the program is to increase understanding of one's self and one's partner along dimensions directly pertinent to the relationship." (page 12). "The term understand as used here . . . refers to the capacity and willingness to appreciate relationship-relevant needs, desires, preferences, aspirations, values, motivations, and emotions of one's own self and one's partners." (page 12) This program is based upon honesty with compassion. Futhermore, Relationship Enhancement (RE) assumes that every person is the expert on him or herself and that each person knows best how he or she perceives things and feels about them. This approach which can be used with individuals or couples, is based on an educational skills-training model. As the learners become skilled in honestly and compassionately expressing their own subjective view of the situation or interaction and how each feels about it they greatly enhances the relationship.

> A recent participant in the RE program stated: "The use of RE in dealing with spirituality was very effective. It's funny how comfortable *we* thought *we* were with *our* views on *our* faith. Not until we decided to use RE did we realize the differences our pathways to spiritual growth were taking. By using RE and allowing the other to *personally* realize what is most important spiritually in our lives, let us realize where we stand, the differences we have, the way to bring those differences together, and how it will allow us to grow together, not only with each other, but with God."[1]

All of our relationships go through stages. The stages of a relationship are beautifully described by Anne Lindbergh in her little book, *Gift from the Sea*. We never stand still. Change is con-

---

[1] The use of RE skills in spiritual growth is the special interest of the Relationship Enhancement Institute, 1035 Locust Avenue, Charlottesville, Virginia 22901, which the author directs.

SOURCES OF HELP

stant. This is true in every area of our life including our spiritual growth.

It is essential to find a counselor who respects your values, your faith and who will listen carefully to both partners. It is essential that the person be competent to help. Pooled ignorance is not helpful! A competent counselor should welcome your questions. Counselors should be willing to state clearly how they will help you, what their qualifications and training are and what credentials they have earned.

The Christian Association for Psychological Studies (CAPS)[2] has a directory of members. The most effective methods for finding a counselor is by talking to others who have gone to a particular counselor and by taking the time and making the effort to talk with several counselors prior to choosing one. I highly recommend that process. I also highly recommend Relationship Enhancement Therapy as the most effective method of marital therapy.

> "Never pull each other to pieces, my brothers. If you do you are judging your brother and setting yourself up in the place of God's Law; you have in fact become a critic of the Law. Yet if you start to criticize the Law instead of obeying it you are setting yourself up as Judge, and there is only one Judge, the One who gave the Law, to Whom belongs absolute power of life and death. How can you

---

[2] It can be obtained from CAPS International, 26705 Farmington Road, Farmington Hills, Michigan 48018.

then be so silly as to imagine that you are your neighbor's Judge?" (James 4: 11-12, Letters)

7
One in Unity

From my studies of the Scriptures in relation to the relationship of marriage for believers, I believe that the husband and wife become one in unity of Spirit. While the following Scripture refers specifically to the body of believers, I believe that it is the clearest explanation of the process of becoming one in the Spirit.

> "For he himself is our peace, who has made the two one and has destroyed the barrier, the dividing wall of hostility, by abolishing in his flesh the law with its commandments and regulations. His purpose was to create in himself one new man out of the two, thus making peace, and in this one body to reconcile both of them to God through the cross, by which he put to death their hostility. He came and preached peace to you who were far away, and to preach to those who were near. For through him we both have access to the Father by one Spirit. Consequently, you are no longer foreigners and

> aliens, but fellow citizens with God's people and members of God's household, built on the foundation of the apostles and prophets, with Christ Jesus himself as the chief cornerstone.
>
> In him the whole building is joined together and rises to become a holy temple in the Lord. And in him you too are being built together to become a dwelling in which God lives by his Spirit. (Ephesians 2: 14-22, NIV)

This emphasis upon oneness in the Holy Spirit is central in all of the passages which refer to the unity of believers. The emphasis upon peace through oneness in God's Spirit is prevalent throughout the Scriptures. This oneness, as so clearly stated in the Scripture above, is based upon the completed work of Jesus Christ. He has reconciled us to God. Our oneness comes about through union with God.

Bruce Narramore states:

> "Our unity with Him is reestablished because our sins have been atoned. No longer do we need to be separated from others because (since our sins and theirs are paid for) we can accept one another without judgment, blame, and condemnation. And we can now experience a deep inner reunification because we ac-

ONE IN UNITY

> knowledge our own inability to close the gap between who we are and who we should be and allow Christ to accomplish that. By accepting the fact that Christ has made us acceptable, His atoning work becomes our point of inner reconciliation and allows us to give up our unrealistic goals, our efforts to satisfy our own judgments through performance and our efforts at self-atonement through guilt feelings. In short we give up our omnipotent, god-like strivings and let God be God." (*No Condemnation*, Ibid, page 224)

Husband and wife, as all believers, become one in unity. Their ultimate purpose, as all creation, is to bring honor and glory to God.

> "Be completely humble and gentle; be patient, bearing with one another in love. Make every effort to keep the unity of the Spirit through the bond of peace. There is one body and one Spirit—just as you were called to one hope when you were called—one Lord, one faith, one baptism; one God and Father of all, who is over all and through all and in all. ... Therefore, each of you must put off falsehood and speak truthfully to his neighbor, for we are all members of one body. In your anger do not sin. Do not let

A SCRIPTURAL GUIDE TO A FULFILLING MARRIAGE

> the sun go down while you are still angry, and do not give the Devil a foothold. ... Get rid of all bitterness, rage and anger, brawling and slander, along with every form of malice. Be kind and compassionate to one another, forgiving each other, just as in Christ God forgave you." (Ephesians 4: 2 ff, NIV)

In Proverbs 10:12 we read:

> "Hatred stirs up dissention, but love covers all wrongs." (NIV)

Stored up, unresolved anger is a destructive force in a relationship. I have heard many different explanations of the reference to anger. Perhaps, it means just what it says. We should not go to bed angry. We should deal with our anger in constructive, honest and compassionate ways. Pretending that we are not angry when we are or feeling guilty about being angry only create further problems. I believe that anger is motivated by fear and/or hurt. The RE skills that I discussed provide a very adequate method for dealing with hurt and fear in constructive ways. It helps individuals take responsibility for their feelings and then helps them to share those feelings with loved ones with compassion and honesty. As a feeling is heard and accepted for what it is—anger, hurt or fear—by the other person, the angry person finds acceptance and understanding. Productive inter-

ONE IN UNITY

actions result in dealing effectively with anger in ways approved by God. Take, for instance, the Scripture which refers to fathers and children:

> "Fathers, do not exasperate your children; instead, bring them up in the training and instruction of the Lord." (Ephesians 6: 4, NIV)

The Greek word for bring them up is *nurture* them in the discipline and admonition of the Lord. The instruction do not exasperate means do not provoke to wrath. There is, therefore, obviously an unacceptable way to express your anger or discipline. Being abusive is that way!

The marriage relationship of believers is given as an illustration of the oneness between Christ and His Church. It is described as an unfolding mystery. We can only experience oneness as we seek after peace and harmony.

A number of years ago, our marriage was in shambles. I left my wife and was planning to divorce her. I was rebellious and very angry at her and at God. During the period of separation, my wife kept praying that God would not only save our marriage but that He would give us one which was beautiful and would be a model for others. I scoffed at the idea and told her she should wake up and face the facts that we had irreconcilable differences. Today, many years later, we are not only together but we are in the process of becoming one in Him. We are blessed beyond our wildest dreams.

A SCRIPTURAL GUIDE TO A FULFILLING MARRIAGE

We have been through very trying times. At times we both felt our hearts would break. During those times, we were able to say, "they meant it to me for harm, but God meant it for good". We have a God of miracles who can break through our unbelief and can take our broken lives and mend them. God can bring beauty out of ugliness. When God changes us, the changes are not cosmetic; they are from within and they are real!

God still speaks differently to my wife and me. How He speaks to each of us is unimportant because God will speak to you in ways appropriate to you. He will speak to you in ways you can understand and accept. As I have written this book, the Holy Spirit of God has spoken to me in powerful and clear ways and the most obvious way has been to bring Scriptural passages to my mind. The greatest heritage that my mother and father gave to me was a knowledge of the Scriptures. I saw my parents studying their Bibles everyday of my life and I was encouraged to study them for myself. When I saw inconsistencies and faults in my parents and in myself, they always encouraged me to study my Bible. That was their greatest love for me.

God's gift to me has been the ability to help others who are struggling to understand and grow. I value His gift and as I have written this book, I have constantly prayed that God would guide me. I have made no attempts to apologize for what the Bible teaches nor have I tried to explain away any passages which I did not under-

ONE IN UNITY

stand or like. I began writing this book when I suffered a professional and personal disruption to my whole way of life. God has in His grace and mercy used that tragedy to reawaken in me a deep desire to serve Him without reservation and without unbelief. This has been a daily moment by moment walk of faith. It is daily communion with God, a daily searching of His Word and it has become a life of prayer without ceasing. My prayer time with my wife each day has become a highlight of every day. Prior to this experience I could not pray out loud. I hated devotions because of my life experiences with them. God has removed those blocks and He has blessed me in such indescribable ways that I am forever thankful to Him and my family. It has been a quiet, inner reformation.

The Holy Spirit has broken through many of my own prejudices and professional biases. He has at times shaken me to the very core of my being. He has at times spoken to me so clearly and so precisely that I cannot doubt His presence in our world today and within me. He has blessed me as I have counseled with people, as I have interacted with my family and as I have contemplated His work in our world today. At times, I have sobbed uncontrollably as I came to understand His love, His mercy and His grace toward me.

We must remember that God is Holy AND that He is Love. As we contemplate His love, we must remember His holiness. As we contemplate

A SCRIPTURAL GUIDE TO A FULFILLING MARRIAGE

His holiness, we must remember His love. He has disciplined me for my rebelliousness and unbelief. Yes, His love is endless and He has forgiven me and restored me to full fellowship. Yes, I have come to know that God is not mocked, for whatsoever a man sows, that shall he also reap. But that is not the end of the story. The end of the story is love and forgiveness and reconciliation. And Jesus said:

> "I tell you that ... there is more rejoicing in heaven over one sinner who repents than over the ninety-nine righteous persons who do not need to repent." (Luke 15: 7, NIV)

It is my wish that you have found hope in these pages. I have found hope and I have found love. God does answer prayer. He, however, will begin that answer in you as you seek to do His will and to love and to seek peace and harmony.

> "Jesus replied: 'Love the Lord your God with all your heart and with all your soul and with all your mind. This is the first and greatest commandment. And the second is like it: Love your neighbor as yourself. All the Law and the Prophets hang on these two commandments." (Matthew 22: 37-40, NIV)

And when all else has failed,
LOVE STILL STANDS.

References

Christenson, Larry (1970). *The Christian Family*. Minneapolis: Bethany Fellowship, Inc. Material cited in the text copyright © 1970 by Bethany Fellowship, Inc. Used by permission.

Duty, Guy (1967). *Divorce & Remarriage*. Minneapolis: Bethany Fellowship, Inc. Copyright © 1967 by Bethany Fellowship, Inc. Used by permission.

Evans, Colleen Townsend (1980). *THE VINE LIFE*. Lincoln: Chosen Books, Fleming H. Revell Co. Material cited in text copyright © 1980. Used by permission.

Gingrich, F. Wilbur (1957). *Shorter Lexicon of the Greek New Testament*. Chicago: The University of Chicago Press. Material cited in the text copyright © 1957. Used by permission.

Guerney, Bernard G., Jr. (1982). *Relationship Enhancement Skill Training Programs for Therapy, Problem Prevention and Enrichment*. San Francisco: Jossey-Bass Publishers. Material cited in this text copyright © 1982. Used by permission.

Keller, W. Phillip (1982). *A Common Man's Quest for God Wonder O'the Wind*. Waco: WORD BOOKS. Material cited in this text copyright © 1982. Used by permission.

Lindbergh, Anne Morrow (1955). *Gift from the Sea*. New York: Random House, Inc. Copyright © 1955. Used by permission.

Moffat, James. *The Holy Bible, A New Translation by James Moffatt*. New York: Harper & Brothers, 1926. Material cited in this text copyright © 1926. Used by permission.

A SCRIPTURAL GUIDE TO A FULFILLING MARRIAGE

Marshall, Alfred (1958). *The R.S.V. Interlinear Greek-English New Testament.* Grand Rapids: Zondervan Publishing House. Material cited in this text copyright © 1958 Editorial Interlination, Samuel Bagster & Sons Ltd. Used by permission.

Narramore, S. Bruce (1984). *No Condemnation Rethinking Guilt Motivation in Counseling, & Parenting.* Grand Rapids: Academie Books. Material cited in this text copyright © 1978 by the Zondervan Corp. Used by permission.

Narramore, Bruce (1978). *You're Someone Special.* Grand Rapids: Zondervan Publishing House. Material cited in this text copyright © 1978. Used by permission.

Phillips, J.B. (1953). *Letters to Young Churches.* New York; The Macmillan Company. Material reprinted with permission. Copyright © 1947, 1948, 1957. Renewed 1975, 1976. Used by permission.

Phillips, J.B. (1972). *The New Testament in Modern English.* New York: The Macmillan Company. Material reprinted with permission. Copyright © 1958, 1960, 1972. Used by permission.

Stuart, Richard B. (1980). *Helping Couples Change A Social Learning Approach to Marital Therapy.* New York: The Guilford Press. Material cited in this text copyright © 1980. Used by permission.

Thompson, Frank Charles (1983). *The Thompson Chain-Reference Bible New International Version.* Grand Rapids: Zondervan Bible Publishers. Material cited in this text copyright © 1973, 1978, 1984. International Bible Society. Used by permission.

Tyndale House Publishers (1971). *The Living Bible.* Wheaton: Tyndale House Publisher. Material cited in this text copyright © 1971. Used by permission.

Vanauken, Sheldon (1977). *A Severe Mercy.* New York: Harper & Row, Publishers, Inc. Material cited in this text copyright © 1977. Used by permission.

Index

Abuse 43, 59, 81-87, 128, 130, 153
Accountability 15-16
Accuser 23
Agreements
    Quid Pro Quo 63
    Holistic 63, 64, 67, 68
Anger 51, 130, 133, 166
Anxiety 28, 35, 88
Appearances 127, 139
Argumentive 61
Biblical Behaviors 125, 127
Change 17, 72, 140, 144
Conformity 144
Counseling 24, 119-152, 161
Discernment 13, 14, 27, 151, 158
Discouragement 21
Divisions 102
Enmeshment 18
Equality & Equity 42, 69, 105
Forgiveness 34, 147, 155, 158, 170
Freedom 28, 29, 31, 35, 72
Gifts 53, 74, 77, 120, 121, 129, 131, 132, 133
God's will 6-7, 26, 35, 77, 126
God's Knowledge 13, 25, 145
Growth xi, 20, 22, 23, 24, 34, 39, 62, 72, 90, 91, 168
Guilt 144
Harmony 29, 71, 88, 97, 103
Head 37, 38, 50, 51, 62, 90, 93
Holy Spirit xi, 5, 7, 13, 23, 28, 32-37, 43-44, 47-48, 54, 56-57, 77-79, 86-87, 89, 101, 111, 116, 120, 121, 123-124, 126, 129, 131-133, 136-138, 143-144, 146, 148, 158, 164-165, 168-169
Humanism 125
Identity 17, 18
Judging 16, 24, 51
Love 20, 22, 26, 30, 32, 33, 60, 66, 97, 134-136, 138-141, 143, 150, 169-170
Mediator 39, 42
Motives 16, 25, 64-65, 127, 130
Nourishment 62, 90
Obedience 5, 7, 15, 29, 34, 36, 65, 72, 111-115
Oneness 12, 20, 26, 28, 29, 42, 163-164, 167
Peace 25, 26, 28, 37, 97, 163
Prayer xi, xii, 23, 34, 35, 130, 169
Repentence 22, 128
Roles 30
Self-love 19
Sexual Relationships 43-45, 58-60, 68, 74-77, 107-108
Sin 33, 82-87, 123, 129, 135-137, 147
Skills 30, 158-161
Spirituality 136-137
Submission 43, 50, 87-106, 115
Unity 28, 33, 37, 45, 71, 164
Victory 25
Wholeness 20, 34
Will 20

CHRISTIAN PARENTS NOW YOU CAN LEARN HOW TO RAISE COMPASSIONATE, CARING, LOVING, DISCIPLINED CHILDREN!

READ:

PARENTING: A SKILLS TRAINING MANUAL
by
LOUISE GUERNEY, Ph.D.

"The most useful book of its kind I've encountered."
Barry Ginsberg, Ph.D.

"Simple language, clear examples and humor..."
Mary O'Connell, Ed.D.

"I can't recommend anything more highly..."
Thomas Vinca, MSW

"Hundreds of evaluations from parents show an overwhelming response from parents... Parenting goes beyond other programs in offering a systematic and down-to-earth approach to solving pressing parent-child difficulties." Andrea Sywulak, Ph.D.

"Of the many parent manuals now on the market, Parenting has the greatest comprehensiveness and continuity." Eric Hatch, Ph.D.

"The inclusion of communication skills, behavior management techniques and decision making strategies... extends to all areas of parent child interactions." Jeanette Coufal, Ph.D.

"Parenting is far more effective than any other parenting program I've tried." Peter Horner, Ph.D.

Send coupon below with payment to: IDEALS, PO Box 391, State College, PA 16804

RETURN FOR FULL-PRICE REFUND
IF NOT COMPLETELY SATISFIED.

☐ Please send me a copy of Parenting: A Skills Training Manual. (Paperback, 151 pages, 6 illustrations).
   I enclose $5.95 and $1.50 for packing and shipping.

Name _____ Address _____

_____ Zip _____